THI
ARGONAUTICA
EXPEDITION

By the same author

OUR TRAVELS
TRAVEL, THAT INCURABLE BUG

THE ARGONAUTICA EXPEDITION

Theodor Troev

Ian Faulkner Publishing

Ian Faulkner Publishing Ltd
Lincoln House
347 Cherry Hinton Road
Cambridge CB1 4DJ

First published by Medicina y Fiscultura, Sofia 1990
This edition first published 1991
© Theodor Troev 1991

All rights reserved. No part of this publication may be reproduced, stored in a retrieval system, or transmitted, in any form or by any means, electronic, mechanical, photocopying, recording, or otherwise, without the prior permission of the copyright owner.

A CIP record for this book is available from the British Library.

ISBN 1-85763-001-7

Printed in Great Britain by Billings and Sons Ltd

CONTENTS

Illustrations	8
Foreword by Tim Severin	11
Introduction by Professor Velizar Velkov	15
1 The Gold Ingot	19
2 *Argonautica*	28
3 Tim Severin and the Jason Voyage	41
4 The Sound of Orpheus's Lyre	52
5 The Crew	75
6 *Aurora* in the Pontus	89
7 Colchis	115
8 Meeting *Argo*	134
9 Homeward Bound	169

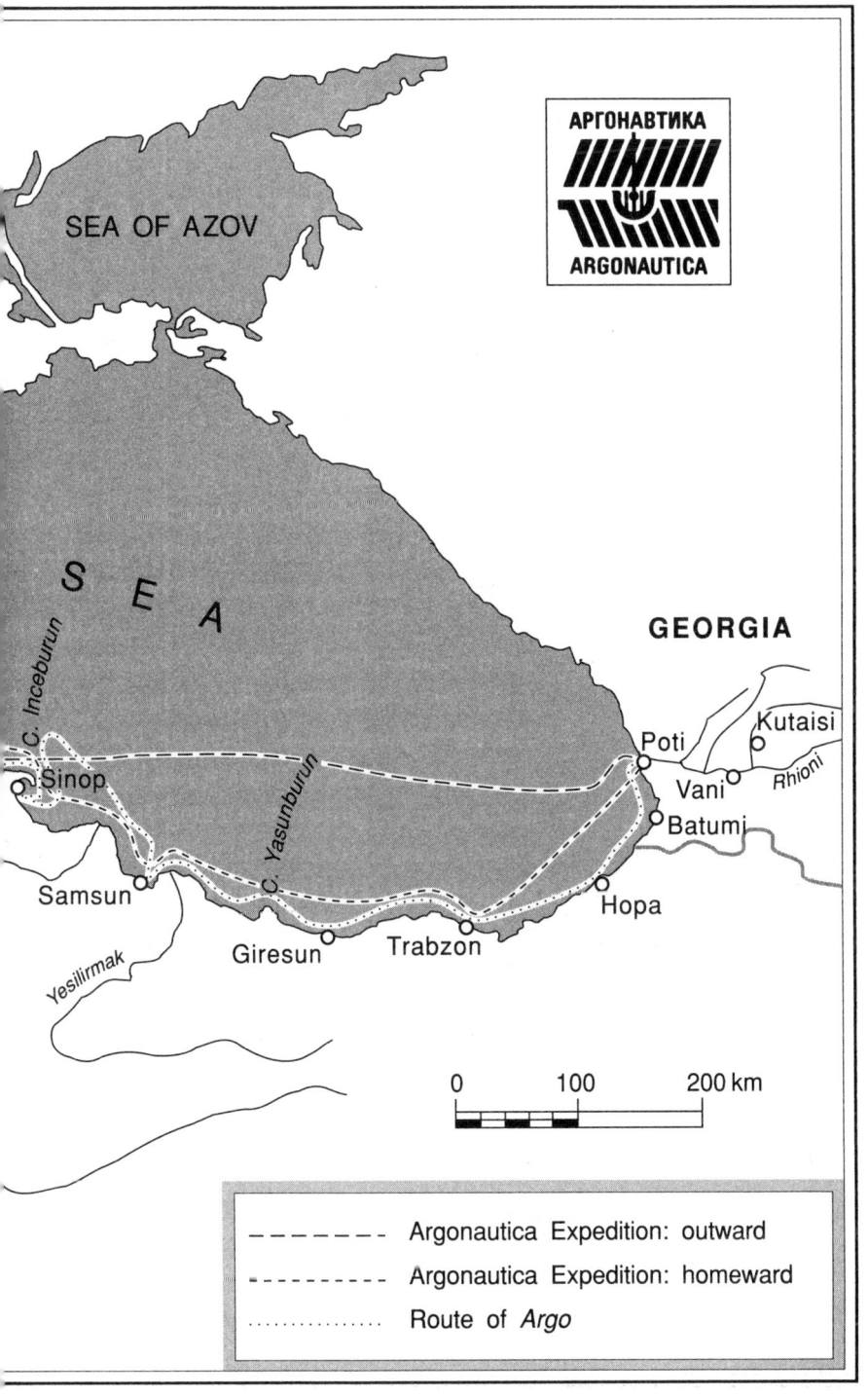

ILLUSTRATIONS

The golden ingot in the shape of a sheepskin discovered in the Black Sea

Stone anchors – evidence of active navigation at the time of the Argonauts

The author and Professor Velizar Velkov

A mural painting on the theme of Jason, Medea and the Argonauts

The flower of Orpheus in the Rhodope mountains

A folk musician in the Rhodope mountains

The Argonautica Expedition setting out from Varna

Tim Severin's *Argo*

The symbolic image of the art of Orpheus presented to the crew of *Argo*

ILLUSTRATIONS

Argo and the Russian training ship *Tovarishch*

The author and Tim Severin

Fair winds for *Argo* on the coast of Georgia

Ruins of a temple near Kutaisi

Example of reliefs found in old Georgian temples

Homeward bound: Mikhail Lazarov with Maria Troev and the author

FOREWORD

by Tim Severin

It was very fitting that my first meeting with Theodor Troev took place on the stern deck of a Bronze Age galley – a replica of a type of vessel that, as far as we can determine, plied the seas at the time when the legend of Jason and the Argonauts was born. The occasion of our first encounter was the arrival of my galley *Argo* on the Black Sea coast of Georgia after her long and arduous journey from Volos in northern Greece, traditional home of Jason himself. It had taken the crew of *Argo* eleven weeks of hard rowing and sailing to cover the distance in the manner of the ancient sailors, creeping our way along the coast from headland to headland, coming ashore to sleep on the beach at night unless – as happened – we were driven out to sea by strong offshore winds and had to survive in a pitching, rolling galley amid the waves and darkness, with the water lapping over the low gunwale and surging back and forth in the bilges. By the time we reached our final landfall on the Georgian coast, *Argo*'s crew had demonstrated beyond refute that such a voyage was practicable. It *could* be done in a vessel of Bronze Age design and construction, and there was no physical or technical obstacle to such a venture. Also, we had tasted at first hand some of the experiences of the early sailors.

At the Georgian port of Poti, we discovered that we had not been alone in our pursuit of the ancient tale of Jason and the Argonauts. There, in connection with the same story, was waiting the Bulgarian team of the Argonautica Expedition aboard their yacht *Aurora*, and Theodor Troev was the team leader. A rubber dinghy brought Theodor to *Argo* and he scrambled aboard, to be introduced and explain how he and his colleagues had also been researching the origins of the Argonaut legend.

In a very real sense, the work of the Bulgarian Argonautica Expedition complements the practical, hand-blistering and muscle-aching endeavours of my own crew of a modern *Argo*. The story of Jason and the Argonauts was composed of many different strands, and several aspects of the ancient legend lay beyond the scope of our research. Theodor and his colleagues, for example, had taken a very special starting-point – the Rhodope mountains of the Balkans. Here, it is said, was the home of Orpheus, a master musician and key member of Jason's team. As the legend of the Argonaut voyage was developed and transmitted down through the generations of bards, Orpheus's role was to become more and more important, until he eventually became a figure to rival even Jason himself. Now, this essential aspect of the legend receives its proper consideration.

Then there is the question of how the Argonauts came back home from Colchis, the land of the Golden Fleece. By what route did they return with the beautiful princess Medea on board and pursued by her vengeful family?

Logic dictates that the fleeing *Argo* could only have returned to Greece by the way she arrived, through the Straits of the Bosphorus. Yet there were writers in the classical world who maintained that Jason and his colleagues sought to escape their pursuers by sailing into the wilderness backwaters of the

FOREWORD

Danube delta, only to be blockaded by the Colchian fleet and forced to continue upstream, until they finally emerged into the Adriatic. So once again there is a tantalising link with the Thracian lands of what is now Bulgaria, and it is from Bulgarian archaeologists and scholars, as well as sailors, that we may find a new interpretation of a puzzling element to the Argonaut legend.

And finally it is my belief that a sea should unite, rather than divide, the people who live around its rim. A Bulgarian seaborne expedition which explores the archaeology and navigation of the Black Sea coasts is illuminating the traces of ancient cultures which all the Black Sea littoral peoples hold in common heritage.

It is a legacy that can be shared and appreciated by all those interested in the background to the earliest voyaging tale in Western literature.

INTRODUCTION

by Professor Velizar Velkov
Director, Archaeological Institute of the Academy of Sciences, Sofia

The story of Jason and the Argonauts is one of the most intriguing of the ancient Greek myths. Recorded by Apollonius Rhodius in his epic poem *Argonautica*, it contains a deep grain of historical fact based on events that happened during the second millennium BC.

The theme of the Argonauts' voyage, which is, among other things, a description of ancient Greek navigation in the Black Sea, has always intrigued students of mythology, literary scholars, archaeologists and historians. The story inspired Tim Severin, the well-known navigator and explorer of myths and legends, to prove the possibility of undertaking such a voyage from Greece to Colchis, or modern Georgia on the east coast of the Black Sea. He supervised a group of Greek shipbuilders who reconstructed a boat similar to those used at the time of Jason, and, with an international crew aboard, accomplished the Jason Voyage. This was an important event as far as studies in this field were concerned.

At the same time, independently of Tim Severin, a group of Bulgarian navigators planned to research the possibility that maritime links had existed between the Bulgarian Black Sea coast and other points on the Black Sea and in the Aegean world. The author of this book, Theodor Troev, was interested in finding out what it really was that the Greeks had sought in the land of the Golden Fleece; it has been assumed that the Golden Fleece symbolised the unknown riches and fertile lands of the Black Sea which attracted merchants and mariners as far back as the second millennium BC.

An interesting discovery made by the Soviet engineer and skin-diver Sergei Kupryanov off Cape Kaliakra on the Bulgarian coast – a gold ingot shaped like an animal hide – gave Theodor Troev the idea of a scientific expedition in the Black Sea. This became known as the Argonautica Expedition, which was joined by Mikhail Lazarov, one of the country's best experts on the Black Sea in classical times, who acted as scientific consultant.

Not only is Theodor Troev an excellent yachtsman and one of the few Bulgarians to take part in major marine scientific expeditions, but he is also a very adept writer. It is no simple matter to organise and head an expedition of the kind described in this book, but it is even more difficult to present the information gained on it in a way which will be understandable to those who were not themselves a part of it. I personally always take pleasure in reading books of this kind, and I consider one of their main functions to be to arouse interest among young people in such voyages of exploration.

The book gives a detailed account of the Argonautica Expedition, which was undertaken at the same time as Tim Severin's Jason Voyage. The whole enterprise was on a considerable scale, with two expeditions starting off at different points and sailing along different routes towards the same destination, finally meeting up in ancient Colchis. The event is an example of scientific collaboration among different countries.

The Argonautica Expedition also aimed to investigate some aspects of navigation in the Black Sea in ancient times. This

INTRODUCTION

question is particularly important to the historiography of the Bulgarian Black Sea coast because, as archaeological studies have revealed, the Bulgarian coast was a busy maritime trading route and played an important role in contacts between the Aegean world and the coastal regions of the Black Sea, which were inhabited by the Thracians.

Scholars of navigation in the time of the ancient Thracians face a number of problems. According to the legend, one of the Argonauts, Orpheus, was Thracian. This fact has always added colour to the story of the voyage undertaken by the Greek heroes, and it indicates that Thracians were involved in maritime trading in the Black Sea.

The Argonautica Expedition also showed how it was possible to sail between two points on the Black Sea coast directly and comparatively quickly. This had hitherto just been a hypothesis based on the fact that maritime traffic had existed between the inhabitants of individual city-states on the western shores of the Black Sea, where Bulgaria is, and on the Asia Minor and northern shores. Links with Colchis during the second millennium BC were shown to have been possible, thus opening the field for the study of mutual influences between the eastern and western shores of the Black Sea. The facts we had already known about intensive maritime traffic between the people inhabiting the western Black Sea coast and the Aegean world were enhanced by additional observations.

Before undertaking his voyage, Theodor Troev did a great deal of preliminary research, studying ancient mythology, navigation in ancient times, and various Bulgarian and foreign works on the subject. The author consulted many historians and archaeologists, who provided him with information that cannot be generally found in works of scholarship. He also presents us with the accounts given by the expedition's scientific director Mikhail Lazarov. Thus the book abounds in information of interest both to the specialist and to the layman.

The results the Bulgarian researchers have achieved by elucidating the possibility of maritime links existing in the second millennium BC between distant regions of the Black Sea are of particular importance. Historians and archaeologists can now use these results in their works and explain the active trade that was carried out among these regions and among individuals and groups inhabiting the Greek city-states. Here again, the gold ingot which the story begins with furnishes unique evidence of the existence of such links.

The success of the Argonautica Expedition, one of the first of its kind in Bulgaria, was great. As leader of the expedition, Theodor Troev was invited by Tim Severin to join him as the only Bulgarian on his subsequent project, the Ulysses Voyage.

I believe this book will appeal to all those who like reading about travel, while the issues it raises will certainly be of interest to classical scholars.

1

THE GOLD INGOT

'Take care of your life, and do not set forth across the ocean's waves in haste;
life is short enough as it is . . .'

Automedontes, first-century Greek poet

Never had I imagined that a piece of metal that had lain at the bottom of the sea for thousands of years could affect the course of the life of somebody living in the late twentieth century.

A fresh breeze was blowing from behind us, filling the mainsail and keeping it taut. Long waves rocked the yacht regularly and noiselessly, while the masts swayed across the star by which I had chosen to keep my bearings. From time to time they would cover it, and then I would try to keep the helm in the same position for as long as I could, imagining that if it was no longer there I must now be sailing towards the sea beyond the *oikoumenos*, as the ancient inhabitants of the Mediterranean called the known world.

I hadn't had such a peaceful night watch for a long time. Beside me in the cockpit sat Sergei, not daring even to move lest he broke the spell of the magical moment. His mind was probably wandering among the megalithic monuments of Malta or plumbing the unexplored depths around the island.

We were returning from a voyage to this tiny island archipelago in the heart of the Mediterranean. The Maltese archaeologists we had met there had filled our heads with all kinds of theories about the place, some going so far as to claim that Malta had once been Atlantis, as it was the westernmost point known to mariners in those times. Another widespread claim was that Ulysses, son of the Argonaut Laertes, was descended from the mythical inhabitants of Atlantis, who in turn had been the first seafarers; or at least that Ulysses had visited the islands during his travels.

On the return journey, a strong wind had forced us to anchor in a harbour on the island of Lesbos. According to legend, it was near this island, home of the sweet-voiced Sappho, that the waves had carried off the head and lyre of the Thracian bard Orpheus, another of the Argonauts, after he had been torn to pieces by the worshippers of Dionysus.

That night we had left behind another legendary island, Lemnos. This was where the Argonauts had had their first adventure during their quest for the Golden Fleece. The women of Lemnos had massacred their husbands for being unfaithful and constantly seducing the beautiful women of Thrace. When Jason and the Argonauts landed here, Queen Hypsipyle nearly managed to talk the heroes into marrying the widows of Lemnos. This would have brought the quest for the Golden Fleece to an ignominious end in sweet voluntary captivity, had it not been for the intervention of Hercules, who reminded his comrades of the real goal of their voyage, and the dishonour that awaited them if they returned without the Golden Fleece.

'Old Hercules must have been out of his mind!' was Sergei's comment when I told him the story. 'Making them leave an island of women just for a couple of gold ingots!'

THE GOLD INGOT

'What do you mean, gold ingots?' I asked, not seeing the connection.

'Haven't I told you my theory about the Golden Fleece yet?' Obviously I didn't know the man as well as I thought I did, even though we had been sharing watches for almost two whole months. Sergei Kupryanov had been born in the Soviet Union, but was a long-standing Fellow of the Bulgarian Academy of Sciences, with dozens of inventions behind him and even more ahead of him. He had a soft spot for women and cats, and didn't like staying in the same place for a long time. He started on many different projects at once, but the surprising thing was that he always managed to finish them. I hadn't for a moment imagined that, along with optics, electronics, cybernetics, video, computers, ecology, skin-diving and yachting (to mention but a few), Sergei had also found the time to ponder on such far-off, hazy subjects as the myth of Jason and the Argonauts and the Golden Fleece.

Sergei settled comfortably into his corner of the cockpit, wrapping a thick fur coat around him. The further north we got in the Aegean, the colder the October nights became.

'When I was a child, I was interested in tales of the sea, even though we lived far away from it – maybe that's what made me so interested in it. Anyway, I lived near a small river, where I learned to swim. Of all the myths and legends I read as a child, the most interesting to me was the myth of Jason and the Argonauts. Even then I dreamed of one day setting out to sea in a wooden ship like *Argo* and sailing to a big river – not like ours – and finding the Golden Fleece. I thought that the most exciting voyage a man could do was to sail in the worlds of ages past. So, after doing various things in my life, I got involved with submarine archaeology – I was a skin-diver, and as an engineer I had worked on the development of several underwater cameras. In this way I took part in various marine expeditions. One of these archaeological trips was to Balchik, where I used every spare moment I had to go diving off Cape Kaliakra. Nobody had told me about it – it was just the cape's legendary fame that attracted me, and its ancient name: Tyrisis. It's got an unusual sound to it, hasn't it? *Ty-ri-sis!* I knew that the area was full of ancient stone anchors and pieces of pottery, and I had a feeling that the place concealed some secret. One day, while diving at about ten metres, I saw a strange-looking object wedged between two rocks. I managed to pull it free, and as I swam towards the surface I noticed that it was quite heavy for its size. It occurred to me that it might be gold – not that I seriously believed it, of course. Back on shore, I got out my knife and scratched it a bit – there was a thin oxidised layer on top, and beneath it there really was the glint of metal. At moments like that, everyone likes to let their imagination run away with them and believe they're on to something really big. I called over my friends who had come with me, saying I'd found sunken treasure. Of course, they laughed. When we got back to Balchik, I showed my find to one of the archaeologists working with us, who wasn't impressed.'

'So what had you actually found, then?'

'Well, at first sight it didn't look like anything special,' Sergei said, spreading his fingers. 'It was a piece of metal, a bit longer than a hand-span – about 25 centimetres long, between 10 and 12 centimetres wide and about a centimetre thick. It had the shape of a double axe-head – narrow in the middle and widening at either end; it wasn't flat, but curled, like a piece of bark or something.'

'And how did you find out that it was made of gold?'

'Well, I just ignored all those who laughed at me, and decided to give it a lab analysis. First of all I did a chemical analysis, and then a structural X-ray analysis, which meant cutting a piece off it, even though I wanted to keep it whole. I remember putting the piece in a vice and scraping it with my penknife to obtain some dust for analysis – it felt as if I was scraping my own hand. Anyway, in the end it did turn out to have some value; it wasn't solid gold, but 32 per cent gold, 18 per cent silver and 43 per cent copper with very small quantities of nickel and sulphur.'

'And how much did your find weigh?'

Sergei laughed. 'They thought me mad when I first got it weighed. You see, there was a greengrocer's nearby. I joined the queue, and when my turn came I simply put it on the scales and asked the woman behind the counter to weigh it. It weighed about one and a half kilograms. Surprised, she asked me what it was. I told her it was gold, and she laughed, and I had to slink away with the rest of the customers giving me funny looks. Later I donated my find to the National Archaeological Museum without asking for anything in return, which to some people's minds confirmed that I was mad. But the greatest reward for me came later, when the archaeologists said that they believed it to be an ingot shaped like a stretched animal hide, and that it might possibly have been a pre-monetary means of exchange, which by analogy would date it to somewhere around the second half of the second millennium BC.'

'You mean the time of the Argonauts?'

'Precisely. That's what really knocked me over. I'd always wanted to find something connected with the Argonauts and the Golden Fleece, and here was a gold ingot in the shape of an animal hide!'

'That must really have got your imagination going!'

'You bet it did. There were so many different theories about what the Golden Fleece had actually been, so one more wouldn't hurt. The most widely held theory is that the Golden Fleece symbolised the sheepskins people once used to pan for gold in the rivers of Colchis. The gold particles in the flowing water would get caught up in the wool, being heavier than water, and later, when the skins were put out to dry in the sun, they really did look as if they were made of gold.'

'And what has all that got to do with your ingot?'

'Well, the ancient goldsmiths who cast these ingots must have deliberately made them in the shape of the sheepskins of Colchis to symbolise the wealth of that region with its gold. Most archaeologists seem to think that the expeditions made in the Black Sea at the time of the Argonauts were in search of metal, which was the mainstay of trade at that time. And here we have a metal ingot in the form of a pre-monetary means of exchange.'

'Are you saying that the Argonauts might have set sail for Colchis in search of gold ingots just like these?'

'Why not? After all, when we speak of the Argonauts today, we usually regard them as a mythical stereotype of early seafarers from Achaean Greece who got as far as the Black Sea.'

'And then, like all real seafarers,' I said, giving Sergei a wink, 'they started spinning incredible yarns, and by ornamenting their tales of their voyage to Colchis created the legend of the Golden Fleece.'

'Something like that,' Sergei said, accepting my statement, and continuing enthusiastically: 'Mythology is mythology after all, but I think that there's always a small grain of truth in everything that the ancients thought up. For example, we know now that in the Aegean world cattle were used as a means of exchange. But, as trade developed, cattle turned out to be too bulky to carry around as coins all the time, so they started exchanging just the hides of the animals. And so later on, when gold ingots made their appearance, wouldn't it have been logical for them to be made in the shape of the animal skins they were designed to replace? Metal ingots like this usually date back to the second half of the second millennium BC, which was when the ancients started exploring the trade routes of the Black Sea, as exemplified in the legend of Jason and the Argonauts.'

'Yes, but have similar objects been found anywhere else, and, if so, what does Cape Kaliakra have to do with Jason's voyage?' I was deliberately egging him on, as I hadn't seen him in such an inspired mood for ages, and was half-expecting him to tell me the exact spot where the Argonauts' ship had actually sunk. I wished one of his colleagues could have seen him then, and afterwards try to tell me that today's scientists and engineers don't have any romantic spirit left!

'Have you read *Archaeology Beneath the Sea* by George Bass?'

'Yes,' I said, not seeing what he was driving at.

'Well, don't you remember the ingots that Bass found off Cape Gelidonya, when he was exploring the wreck of a Bronze Age ship – one of the oldest to be found at the bottom of the sea? They had a shape similar to the one I found at Kaliakra, except that they were made of copper and each weighed just under 30 kilograms. Copper ingots similar to mine have also been found in Egypt, Cyprus, Crete, Mycenae, Euboea and the Adriatic Sea. And do you know the comparison drawn by the Bulgarian archaeologist Mikhail Lazarov? He worked out that the value of the Kaliakra Ingot, calculated in talents, which were a unit of weight in the Aegean world, is greater than all the 34 copper ingots found in Gelidonya put together. So it obviously can't have been just any old ship that had sailed past Cape Kaliakra with such a precious cargo aboard.'

'What ship sailing past Cape Kaliakra?'

'Well, any old Achaean ship. But for argument's sake, let's call her *Argo*, returning with her cargo of ingots along one of the Black Sea trading routes. At Kaliakra she might have been overtaken by a storm, causing the crew to throw overboard some of her valuable cargo – partly to appease the gods, and partly to lighten the ship's load. Apart from that, in one of the classical versions of *Argo*'s return journey from Colchis, the ship is described as heading for the Istros, which is the Danube, from the southern Black Sea, which would mean that it really did pass Cape Kaliakra.'

'Have you ever told any of this to marine archaeologists or historians?'

'Not everything, because I didn't want to be laughed at. It seems that people don't like to let their imaginations run away with them if they don't have any concrete evidence to base their ideas on; and I haven't yet found the remains of a ship with the name *Argo* inscribed on it, nor have I found ingots stamped 'Golden Fleece' or 'Made in Colchis'. Basically, scholars regarded the Kaliakra Ingot as a one-off thing in world archaeology, since most of the ingots discovered so far have been homogeneous in composition, and are usually made of copper. So it isn't really possible to draw any definite conclusions. I just regard my theory as a working hypothesis, which will one day be either proved or disproved. I'd be interested to hear what the archaeologists of Georgia, for example, would have to say in the light of their studies of the eastern Black Sea, ancient Colchis.'

Dawn was breaking. Beyond the stern, the Isle of Lemnos was now scarcely visible. We were heading for the Dardanelles, the ancient Hellespont, which also owes its name to the story of the Golden Fleece: when Phrixus and Helle were flying across the straits on the golden-fleeced ram that their mother, the goddess Nephele, had sent to save them from being sacrificed by their stepmother Ino, Helle dozed off and fell into the sea, which was subsequently named in her honour. So Phrixus reached Colchis by the Black Sea alone, sacrificed the ram to Zeus and presented the fleece to Aeetes, king of Colchis. The

Golden Fleece remained in a cave guarded by a dragon until the Argonauts arrived in Colchis and Jason succeeded in stealing the fleece, helped by Aeetes' daughter, the sorceress Medea.

For thousands of years historians and scholars have been interested in the myth of the Golden Fleece and the voyage of the Argonauts, because it contains interesting descriptions of the peoples and places the *Argo* passed on her voyage. Some of these places were in ancient Thrace. In addition, the actual voyage of the Argonauts through the Bosphorus is regarded as a description of the first exploration of the distant sea beyond the known world made by Mediterranean seafarers. Was it possible that we could add something to the many studies and hypotheses that had been raised about those mythological times?

'Sergei, what do you say about an expedition to some of the places which the Argonauts visited?'

I had no idea that this suggestion, made almost as a joke as we entered the Dardanelles in the spectral gloom of that chilly October morning, would turn the following years of my life into a real adventure.

2
ARGONAUTICA

The best thing about an expedition is dreaming about it.

The yearning to get up and set off on a journey is never as strong as at the moment when, from the hazy mist of the original idea, a star suddenly lights up and shows you the way. At that stage you are still in control – the journey is clear only in a most general way, like a general outline, leaving your imagination free to invent as many variations as you please. You sit poring over maps with your friends and discussing various possible routes, overcome entirely by a sense of adventure. You meet scholars who reveal entirely new worlds to you, and your whole being feels charged with the creative energy that the dream of travel brings.

Then in the dreamy haze another star shines, followed by another, and another ... until the whole route is quite clear to you and you start seeing the details and the snags that might crop up. So everything has to be meticulously planned. One by one the different variants are crossed off the list, until in the end there is just one single one left – maybe not the one you originally dreamed of, but the most realistic one, given the position of the stars at that specific moment. From then on, the journey controls you. It is master of the situation and leads you on by its own iron rules; it makes you bend down at the smallest snag, which you have to push aside if you want to take the next step. Then at one point your back starts aching so much that you feel like just kicking the whole lot aside, and to hell with the consequences! But then you stop to look back, and see that you're not alone. There are others counting on you, and you realise that you can't let your temper run away with you. So what you have to do then is to bend over again, remove the next snag and make sure that it won't spring back. The most important thing at moments like that is not to forget what you set out for, to remember the dream that inspired it all.

When Sergei and I got back from our trip to Malta, we spent months in that initial sweet, hazy phase of dreaming about our future expedition. I spent hours with friends from the UNESCO Scientific Expeditions Club (SEC) looking at charts of the Black Sea, the ancient Pontus, and wondering how to tie the idea in with studies of 'Thracia Pontica', or rather maritime Thrace; for Thracian tribes inhabited not just the shores of the Black Sea, but also the northern Aegean and the approaches to the Black Sea – in other words, a significant proportion of the places which the Argonauts passed on their voyage.

It was also time to choose a historian or archaeologist to act as the research co-ordinator of the future programme. We asked the board of the SEC what they thought.

'Velizar Velkov is the man you need!' said Boyan Manev categorically. Boyan had for years been taking part in the expeditions of the Cosmos Submarine Research Team of the SEC. He knew Professor Velkov well from many of Cosmos's undertakings.

'Yes, Velkov would be quite suitable,' said Yavor Bankov of the Institute of Monuments of Culture. 'He supports anything that might be useful to history and archaeology, and he's not the kind to limit himself to one field, but has an all-round view on many things.'

'You won't catch him shutting himself up in an ivory tower,' Sergei concluded characteristically. 'If you've ever seen how he jumps with delight at the tiniest discovery on an expedition you'll know that he's the man for us.'

And so the scales tipped in favour of Professor Velizar Velkov, director of the Academy of Sciences Archaeological Institute and Archaeological Museum, head of Sofia University's Ancient and Medieval History Department and chairman of the National Committee of the World Council of Museums. By this stage the professor, so respected and loved by all members of the club, was practically the only one who didn't know that he had been chosen for the job of chief scientific co-ordinator of a prospective SEC expedition. An expedition whose name we didn't even know yet.

So, as the initiator of the idea for the programme, it was up to me to put the matter to the professor in such a way that he wouldn't be able to refuse.

From the original overall idea of the expedition and all the different variants it offered, I drew one thread that connected the gold Kaliakra Ingot and the routes of Late Bronze Age navigators in the Black Sea to Colchis, and the kingdom of Aeetes where the Golden Fleece was kept. I put it all together in a project which I rewrote about ten times. I had to delve through a great deal of scientific literature in order to be able to present the idea in the best light on the one hand and, on the other, to make it as brief as possible.

We presented the project to Professor Velkov in the Archaeological Institute. On the following nights my sleep alternated between sweet dreams and nightmare visions. Either they were fabulous visions of us all sailing off in a yacht rigged with an ancient square sail, or nightmares of the venerable professor, in front of all my friends from the Scientific Expeditions Club, with a malicious smile on his face, presenting me with a medal shaped like the gold ingot which turned out to be made of pumpkin. And then I would wake up.

At long last the reply came on a sheet of paper with an Archaeological Institute letterhead. I let Sergei read it first, my eyes impatiently on his hands.

... your material was extremely interesting. The ingot you mention is indeed one of the most valuable and interesting finds made during submarine studies off the Black Sea coast. The facts you give about the ingot and the analogies you draw are precise and coincide with the latest views Bulgarian scholarship has on the question. The hypothesis you raise concerning the origins of the ingot seems legitimate.

The Archaeological Institute believes that the expedition you propose will contribute towards the elucidation of a number of questions of ancient culture along the Bulgarian coast. In our view you raise important academic questions.

It would be appropriate for the route of the sailing expedition to follow one used by ancient navigators, possibly Varna–Eregli–Sinop–Poti. As scientific director of the expedition we propose Mikhail Lazarov, a senior research assistant who has a number of publications in this field.

Underneath was Professor Velkov's signature.

A few days later, Sergei and I were in Professor Velkov's office. As soon as we came in, Velizar Velkov gave us his beaming cordial smile, looking as if we'd promised to bring him the Golden Fleece itself from Colchis.

'You're just in time! Another Argonaut who's sailing with you has just arrived from Varna. Just a minute, while I call him...'

A minute later a man came into the office. He was about fifty, but his hair was already growing white; he was thick-set, and around my height, which is about medium, possessing a lively gait and the healthy, weather-beaten and somewhat rugged face of a man who spends most of his time outdoors. His scowling eyebrows and frowning lips were in marked contrast with Professor Velkov's prepossessing smile.

I stole a glance towards Sergei. 'It's old Misho!' he whispered, just as the Professor started introducing us to the knit brows, while the two narrow eyes beneath stared penetratingly at me. Before us was the prospective scientific director of the expedition Mikhail Lazarov, an archaeologist from the coastal city of Varna and chairman of the Council of Experts of the Maritime History and Submarine Archaeology Centre, Sozopol. I only knew him from his remarkable book, *The Sunken Flotilla*, a highly readable account of submarine research off the Black Sea coast and its contribution to the ancient history of the Pontus.

'Professor Velkov has told me about your project,' Mikhail Lazarov began in a flat tone and an expression on his face which betrayed neither approval nor disapproval. Suddenly he asked me a question: 'Do you know that some years ago there was an experimental yachting cruise along some of the ancient Black Sea navigation routes?'

'If I'm not mistaken,' I answered as casually as possible, given the fact that starting off on the right foot was paramount if the expedition was to get on with its scientific director, 'you're referring to the experiment carried out by Assen Dremdjiev and Dimiter Klissourov with the yacht *Vega*. Their aim was to test the hypothesis that ancient craft sailing from Sinop to the north and north-western coast of the Black Sea could, instead of following the traditional coastal route, cut straight across from Inceburun to Cape Sarich, which is the narrowest part of the Black Sea.' I felt Lazarov's eyes light up, and went on with greater confidence: 'Although as far as I know, the question of when the ancients mastered this route is still under debate. Some historians believe that it was discovered during the sixth century BC, while others estimate the fourth or even the second century BC, which would make it much later than the Argonauts' voyage.'

'That's right,' Sergei joined in, giving away the source of my information on the matter, 'Assen Dremdjiev was also captain of our yacht on our voyage to Malta, and he told us what a hard time he had trying to see both the northern and the southern coasts of the Black Sea from half-way, as he should have, according to Strabo.'

'In fact, as you were scientific adviser on Dremdjiev's expedition, it wouldn't be anything new for you,' I said, looking at Lazarov. I noticed his puckered brows relaxing a little.

'Although of course this will be the first time we're mounting a yachting expedition of such length,' Professor Velkov intervened. 'Oh, I wish I were a little younger and a little less busy so I could go with you! None of us has visited the Asia Minor coast yet, although we've written reams of articles about its ancient history. Oh well, at least Lazarov will get the chance to see it – and not just from the land, but from the sea as well.'

Then he opened a chart of the Black Sea with the ancient names of harbours on it.

'Misho and I decided on this proposed route for our expedition,' he said, tracing with his finger the route Varna–Eregli–Sinop–Samsun–Poti, 'so that it will cover the Argonauts' voyage in the Black Sea right up to the finish in Phasis, today the river Rhioni near Poti. On the southern coast, your main stops will be Sinope, nowadays Sinop, which is the oldest Miletan colony on the Black Sea, then Amisos, today Samsun, another colony of Miletus, and finally Trapezund, a colony of Sinope.'

'But let's get one thing clear,' Mikhail Lazarov said finally. 'Whenever the journey of the Argonauts in the Black Sea is mentioned, it is usually assumed that the legend is a reflection of the initial exploration of the Black Sea basin by navigators from the Mediterranean. But my many years of underwater archaeology have convinced me that the voyage of the Argonauts was just one more voyage in the Pontus, not the first. The trouble with all claims that navigation first emerged in the Pontus during the period of the great Greek Colonisation in the sixth and seventh centuries BC is that they regard Black Sea navigation as something introduced there by peoples living outside the Black Sea region. They seem to overlook the fact that sailing is impossible without shores and coasts, and it can't be taken in isolation from life on shore. As Professor Velkov, as one of the pioneers of submarine archaeology in Bulgaria, will be the first to confirm, uninterrupted human habitation of the Black Sea coast resulted in the use of the sea as a means of communication both within the Black Sea and with the Mediterranean.'

I glanced at Sergei – he, too, was all ears, like a student at a lecture.

'The task that we have to set ourselves on our expedition,' he went on – and I realised from his use of the word 'our' that he was already one of us – 'is to try to study some concrete evidence of this millennium of navigation in the Black Sea. We'll have to try to re-create the ancient shipping routes, study old ports and harbours, currents, winds, weather patterns, and so forth. Did the ancients really confine themselves to coastal navigation, or did their captains have the skill and courage to cross the Black Sea directly? How did they actually navigate? There are so many unanswered questions. We'll be able to look for some of the answers on this expedition, while the others will have to be part of a longer-term research programme.'

When the 'lecture' was over, I decided to set the record straight.

'Have you sailed before?' I asked.

'No, only in motorboats and small boats along the coast on submarine expeditions,' said Lazarov, looking at me. 'If it's seasickness you're bothered about, you needn't have any worries on that count.'

Right from this moment, we were on 'Misho' and 'Theo' terms. Misho turned out to be of the right stuff for a yachtsman. His many years in submarine archaeology had evidently given him a fine sense of how far an experiment can go and how to strike a sensible balance between scientific research and the practicalities of a marine expedition.

Thus far, however, we had only been sailing in the seas of history, and like a true captain, Professor Velkov steered us from one scholar to another so that we could gradually take on the theoretical cargo our imaginary ship needed for the expedition.

'You must go and see Zlatozara Gocheva of the Thracian Studies Institute!' the professor told me once over the phone. 'I've talked with her and she's prepared to see you and help you. At the moment, Zara's working on a translation of Apollonius's *Argonautica*, and she's found some interesting references to Thracian culture in some part of the epic.'

This was just what I wanted, because at the moment I was trying to hack my way through the 5,835-verse *Argonautica* in Russian translation; the translator had tried to convey the poetry and pathos of the original by using the Russian language rather than keeping as close to the original as possible for the sake of scholarship and at the cost of the poetry. Perhaps he was trying to reflect the fact that Apollonius was a poet and academic rolled into one, or rather that he was a learned poet, which was usual in the Hellenic era.

That is what makes Apollonius's *Argonautica* such a valuable source of information for anyone interested in a more detailed account of Jason's voyage to Colchis; it is also the fullest version of the story which has come down to us. *Argonautica* remains a classic reference work, even though it was written somewhere in the mid third century BC, which is actually a whole millennium after the Argonauts' voyage. That is, if we accept that it took place one generation before the Trojan War.

Zara Gocheva received me in her study at home, which was packed so full of books that there was only room for a single chair and a table with a typewriter and a bed in the corner. Right from the start of our conversation, as I was explaining to her the idea of our expedition, I realised with joy that she, like the ancient authors she translated, was also partial to the idea of combining academic work with poetry and romance.

'If you want to feel the distinctive style of Apollonius's *Argonautica*,' she said, showing me a fat volume in ancient Greek, you should get a better idea of the author of the epic. As you know, he spent a great deal of his life in his native city of Alexandria, which was the capital of the Ptolemaic Kingdom. If we believe one of the biographers whose works have survived to this day, he started writing poetry at a comparatively advanced age. So, with him, the academic precedes the poet. He was a pupil of the academic poet Callimachus, who originated what is known as the Alexandrian trend in poetry and was declared the father of bibliography, as he compiled a catalogue of the works contained in the huge Alexandrian library. This detailed literary historical study alone consisted of 120 volumes. So you can imagine what a colossal amount of reference books Apollonius had to work with . . .'

'And Apollonius himself worked as chief librarian at Alexandria too, didn't he? Then wouldn't he have had access to all the information that had been accumulated until then to write his *Argonautica*?'

'He certainly would. The ancients also say that the dispute

between the two poets, which forced Apollonius to leave Alexandria and settle in Rhodes – hence his name Apollonius Rhodius – was about whether or not it was possible to write a heroic epic poem in the style of Homer's epos.'

'To be honest, when I tried to read the Russian translation of *Argonautica*, I didn't really get the feeling that I was reading anything in the style of Homer's epos . . .'

'Well, that's the whole problem. Despite his attempts to continue Homer's epic poems and to give a coherent mythological account of the Argonauts through his own epic, Apollonius is very different from Homer, and retains many features characteristic of the poetry of the Hellenic period. For example, in giving his chronological account of the Argonauts' voyage – starting with their preparations, the voyage, the capture of the Golden Fleece and ending with the return journey – he often breaks the continuity of the narrative by adding notes which he culled from different legends of various periods. This "scholarly" aspect of Apollonius's epic shows us that he had a different attitude towards mythology and its significance.'

'Meaning?'

'Meaning above all that, true to Hellenic thinking and the Hellenic world-view, he isn't just interested in the straight story of the heroes and their adventures. The myth upon which *Argonautica* is based tells us of events which happened in deep antiquity. They are things which happened before the Trojan War. They reflect elements of the earliest history, not just of Greece, but of the Mediterranean world, the Aegean islands, Asia Minor and the Black Sea as a whole. These were all things that happened before the Trojan War. The legend of the Argonauts doesn't only reflect the earliest period of maritime history in the Mediterranean and Aegean, but also the penetration of the Black Sea and the exploration of its coast, which must also have happened at quite an early stage. That is why Apollonius's *Argonautica* is so important to us and the study of Thracian culture – not just on mainland Greece, but also elements of that culture on the Aegean islands and along the northern coast of Asia Minor, which the Argonauts all passed on their voyage to Colchis. Apollonius tries to cram in a number of different legends of this part of the world, descriptions of cities, the exploits of local heroes, and so forth. In the spirit of all Hellenic poets and their times, he shows a special interest in the culture's ancient roots which set it apart from classical Greek culture. They sought their links with the East and Asia Minor, which at that time were considered to have played an important role in the emergence of Hellenic culture. Apollonius concentrates on previous mythological conceptions of the inhabitants of Asia Minor, tracing their roots right to the time of the Argonauts. What interests us are these references in the epic, and its relation to what we know about Thrace and its culture . . .'

'Yes, but Apollonius did write his *Argonautica* ten whole centuries after the supposed time of the Argonauts' voyage. Do we know exactly what he used as references when describing the actual voyage?'

'We don't know exactly how much Apollonius himself knew, although quite a lot of authors had already written about *Argo* and her voyage, or at least made references to it.'

Zara Gocheva reached out and produced a volume with a brown cover, and promptly started reading from it:

> Only one ship has passed there unharmed – its name is familiar to all – *Argo* – which then returned from Aeetes. A wave would have smashed the ship on a reef, were it not for Hera, Jason's protectress . . .

'The *Odyssey*, when they pass through the Planktes?' I said, in response to her questioning look.

'That's right. And, apart from mentioning *Argo* in the *Odyssey*, Homer writes in the *Iliad* about Jason's son from Hypsipyle, the queen of Lemnos; he ruled Lemnos at the time of the Trojan War, and he supported the Greeks in an ambush. So some authors conclude that, if Jason's son was on the throne at the time when Troy fell, his father as leader of the Argonauts must have visited Lemnos one generation earlier.'

'So, if the Trojan War took place between 1250 and 1200 BC, or as most archaeologists claim today, around 1225 BC, the voyage of Jason and the Argonauts must have taken place somewhere in the middle of the thirteenth century BC.'

Zara Gocheva again referred to her brown book:

'We don't know whether Apollonius had access to other texts by Homer besides the *Odyssey* and *Iliad*, as Strabo later says that Homer also described places "around the Propontus and the Pontus Euxinos all the way to Colchis, the goal of Jason's voyage". But, apart from being better informed than us, Apollonius's epic was also aimed at a more informed audience than us, relying on a lot of prior knowledge among his readers. That is why it wasn't very clear to his later researchers. And it led to a wide range of differing comment even in antiquity, which for its part tells us a lot about the legends and the versions of the legend which the author relies on; it also tells us how knowledgeable ancient authors were on these matters, and gives us a new angle on the myths of the age.'

'And do you think that these comments will be useful for our expedition?'

'I certainly do. If we compare the facts given in the epic with ancient commentary on it, we'll be able to verify many of the details given in *Argonautica* about Thracian culture – or at least the Thracians inhabiting the regions through which Jason and the Argonauts travelled.'

After my first meeting with Zara Gocheva I returned home

with a file full of documents: it was a copy of her partial translation of *Argonautica*. I put it down on my desk, and beside it opened the new diary I'd bought for the expedition.

On the cover of the diary I wrote in large letters: ARGONAUTICA EXPEDITION, and immediately wrote on the first page:

> The expedition's name, *Argonautica*, embraces several of its aspects: the contacts that existed between the ancient inhabitants of Thracia Pontica and the rest of the Black Sea and the Aegean, which are expressed in the myth of Jason and the Argonauts, and the symbolic sense of the word *Argonautica*, which implies the discovery of new and unknown worlds, which was just as much a part of the human spirit in ancient times as it is now.

The expedition had begun. We still had to plan a schedule for our voyage to Colchis, taking care to remove as many organisational snags beforehand as possible.

I wasn't in any particular hurry; I wanted to prepare everything carefully, down to the last detail. Then a piece of news from Ireland made me realise that the moment had come, and there was no time to lose.

3

TIM SEVERIN AND THE JASON VOYAGE

People have always been inclined to see coincidences as the finger of Fate, believing that this finger shows them the way to go.

I myself have never been a fatalist, but what happened on that sunny winter's day really did make me think that the time for our Argonautica Expedition had come. A year earlier, and it would have been too early. A year later, and it would have been too late.

I was having a coffee with Tinko Trifonov in the Green Room of the Crystal Café in Sofia. Tinko is perhaps the most yachting-mad journalist in Varna, constantly keeping up to date with the press and the yachting magazines received by the Captain Georgi Georgiev Yacht Club, Varna. He never missed a single item on competitions, voyages or expeditions. He had come to Sofia for a day to visit some enthusiasts who wanted to start up a Bulgarian sea magazine – the future *Morski Svyat* (*Nautical World*) – and during my lunch hour the two of us were toying with ideas for the future magazine, also wondering what kind of expeditions such a magazine could lend its support to. I happened to mention the Argonautica Expedition to him, as something that at the moment was far off in the future, with much preparation still ahead. Tinko was thoughtful.

'Theo, I'd be telling you a lie if I said I remember where I read it, but someone's preparing to sail along the route taken by Jason and the Argonauts from Greece to Colchis. And they're building an exact replica of *Argo* on a Greek island ...'

'Did it say when they're starting?' I interrupted eagerly.

'It'll be quite soon, actually. They're going to give the ship a trial run this spring, and then start the voyage straight afterwards.'

'And who's the mastermind behind the whole experiment?'

Tinko paused, and then said: 'Tim Severin!', as if he wanted to see the effect his words would have.

They certainly did have an effect. After Thor Heyerdahl, the prominent Norwegian explorer, Tim Severin was the most outstanding figure in voyages aboard reconstructions of ancient craft. Not ten years had passed since the news of his Brendan Voyage had made him famous among all lovers of seaborne adventure. With a small crew in a small ox-hide craft he had crossed the North Atlantic to test the hypothesis that Irish monks had reached the shores of America centuries before Christopher Columbus. The hypothesis was based on an ancient manuscript, *Navigatio Sancti Brendani Abattis*, which described a voyage made by St Brendan, an Irish missionary of the sixth century.

When Tim Severin's subsequent bestseller, *The Brendan Voyage*, was not yet translated into Bulgarian, reports started appearing about his next major expedition. Called the Sindbad Voyage, it was to follow in the track of Sindbad the Sailor with the aim of sifting out the grains of truth that lay behind the tales of his travels in the *Thousand and One Nights*. After building a copy of a medieval Arab sailing-ship, Severin set out with a crew of twenty from Europe, America and Arabia along the traditional trading-routes from Oman to China via India, Sri Lanka, Sumatra and Singapore. His 6,000-mile voyage in a ship whose hull was 'sewn' together with coconut-hair ropes instead of being nailed together, took him almost eight months.

And now, after the Atlantic and Indian oceans, Tim Severin was preparing a voyage which would take him near to where we were – the Black Sea. It would be unforgivable to miss the chance of meeting him, even if it meant pushing ourselves really hard to get there on time. If Tinko's information was correct, we didn't have much time. The trouble was, he couldn't give me any details – he didn't know where *Argo* was being built ('on a Greek island' had been the rather general remark), nor did we know when it would start ('after the trial run this spring' was also rather vague), nor where we could get hold of Tim Severin, who might be somewhere in the Greek islands or back in Ireland, which had become his home several years before.

Immediately after my conversation with Tinko I phoned Sergei. When I told him the news, there was a silence at the other end of the line. I was just wondering if I had been cut off when such a choice Russian oath thundered in the earpiece that made me jump back and look around to make sure that nobody else had heard him. It was the first time I had heard Sergei swear.

'And what'll we do, now that he's got in there first?' he said, mixing Bulgarian and Russian in emotion. 'So he builds an *Argo*, does he? And our expedition – finished!'

I couldn't understand his reaction.

'Why on earth should we give up? No, now we've got to get Argonautica moving as quickly as possible so that we can meet up with him somewhere in the Black Sea.'

'What a good idea! Of course, we join forces!' said Sergei,

sounding delighted. 'We'll think about it at your place this evening!'

On the way home I met Peter Beron, one of Bulgaria's greatest travellers. He had been on Bulgarian and international expeditions to more than fifty different countries. It was like a good omen. I mentioned the idea of meeting Tim Severin.

'I can't help you there, because I don't know his whereabouts,' said Beron, shaking his long beard, 'but don't give up! You'll think of something in the end. When the bird lands on your shoulder, grab it before it can fly off again!' He put his hand on my shoulder as if initiating me into the order of travellers, and rushed off about his business.

In the evening Sergei burst into my flat triumphantly brandishing a magazine. He had gone through all the magazines received in the Soviet Scientific Centre since the New Year, and in the latest issue of the travel magazine *Vokrug Sveta* (*Around the World*) had found an article entitled, 'To Colchis aboard the New *Argo*'. It was about Tim Severin's planned voyage.

I grabbed the magazine from his hands, eagerly devouring the article:

> At the moment Tim Severin, combining his precision as a historian with his expertise as a shipwright, is preparing a new voyage. This will be called the 'Voyage of the Heroes' and will over two consecutive years incorporate his Jason Voyage and the Ulysses Voyage.
>
> The Jason Voyage will begin in Iolcos, today the port of Volos, crossing the northern Aegean and passing the islands of Lemnos, Samothraki and Gokceada to the Hellespont (Dardanelles). They will sail through the Propontus (Sea of Marmara) and up the Bosphorus, where the Symplegades almost crushed *Argo*, after which the prow of the ship will cut through the waves of the Pontus. Then comes the land of the Amazons, i.e. the Black Sea coast of Asia Minor and further east towards the land of the

Chalybes, which are just a stone's throw from Colchis. There are also the fertile fields of Phasis, which is what the ancient Greeks called the river Rhioni, and the city of Aeae – could the present town of Poti be on its site? That is the route which Tim Severin intends to travel this year in order to piece together the fragments of Jason's voyage which we know from ancient authors, and to compare the landscape given in ancient literature with the present-day landscape. He will piece together and compare as only he can – by sailing on a replica of an ancient Greek ship.

'And *Argo* is nearly ready!' said Sergei, looking over my shoulder, even though he had read the article several times already, as happy as a child about to get a new toy.

In my excitement, I started reading it aloud:

The ship is almost ready; its construction was begun last autumn. It is a twenty-seat galley, of the kind that was widely used in ancient times for exploration and convoys. The measurements and design have been checked with historical sources and ancient depictions. It will be about 16 metres long, almost 3 metres wide, its draught will be just 30 centimetres, and its displacement between 5 and 6 tonnes. The area of its rectangular sail will be 28 square metres. The modern Argonauts will steer their craft with the help of two steering-oars fixed to the side of the ship.

Sergei was becoming more and more impatient. 'Read further down, look, here!' he said, indicating the final paragraphs.

Tim Severin is picking an international crew. The vessel will be launched in spring, and in May it will set sail in the open sea. If everything goes according to plan, in early summer the travellers will have the Sea of Marmara behind them, in June they will sail past Turkish shores, stopping off at all places which the legendary

THE ARGONAUTICA EXPEDITION

Argo visited, reaching Colchis and the mouth of the river Rhioni by the end of July.

Next year, the 'Voyage of the Heroes' will continue. Aboard the same ship, Tim Severin will sail for four months in search of the places which Ulysses visited during his travels.

Let us wish him success in his undertakings. And that in Colchis he will find his Golden Fleece, the Golden Fleece that every historian looks for: confirmation of his hypotheses.

'So we'll be in Colchis in July!' Sergei announced. Then he laughed. 'We can take Severin a photo of our ingot. Just imagine – him going to look for a Golden Fleece in Colchis, and we bring him one from Thrace. What a laugh!'

'OK – joking aside, let's think about how we can get in touch with Severin and find out some more about his programme. After all, we can't spend the whole of July hanging around in Georgia waiting for him to turn up.'

'You're right. There's no joking with the Georgians. In one month they'll get us so drunk that we'll forget what we came for. Especially when they know that we're also after the Golden Fleece – they'll intoxicate us right out of our minds.'

'That's why we must find out when the Jason Voyage expects to reach Poti. If *Vokrug Sveta* have such a detailed article about it, they must know when Tim Severin and *Argo* are expected to enter Soviet waters.'

'I imagine that the machine for organising his reception has already been put into motion. Well, there's no point in wondering. Better just write a letter to *Vokrug Sveta*. I bet they'll be interested to hear that two Argonaut expeditions will be arriving in the same year.'

As Sergei sat down to compose a letter in Russian, I remembered that some years ago I had met Maurice Harmon, a professor of Irish literature at Dublin University. I decided to drop him a line, as he would probably have heard about Tim Severin's expedition and would be able to tell me something.

Sergei left at midnight. After the excitement of the day I couldn't get to sleep. A series of repeated images from the day kept running through my mind, images that wouldn't fade away quickly: Tinko with his calm smile – 'And they're building an exact replica of *Argo* on a Greek island . . .'; then Peter Beron's beard and his hand on my shoulder – 'When the bird lands on your shoulder, grab it before it can fly off again!' Sergei, triumphantly holding aloft his copy of *Vokrug Sveta* – 'And *Argo* is nearly ready!' I also remembered when I had first seen Tim Severin's book *The Brendan Voyage*. It was the first time I was taking a yacht out to sea in winter. The waves were giving the fibreglass shell a hard time, and I could really imagine what it must have been like aboard the ox-hide *Brendan* in the rough seas of the Atlantic.

Now I was being rocked to and fro by excitement at the chance of meeting Tim Severin in person. He and Thor Heyerdahl were to me like legendary figures towering high above everyday life. They were like characters from adventure stories. It was impossible for me to picture Tim Severin in the flesh, talking to me, not to mention myself in his galley!

Then I started wondering how Tim Severin himself would react to meeting an expedition that had a lot in common with his. What might interest him most about collaborating with us? To what extent would his latest expedition combine research and adventure, as the Brendan and Sindbad Voyages had done?

I switched on my bedside light and took out my copy of *The Brendan Voyage*. I looked through the photos of Tim Severin. He had the lean face of a not very robust man, a mouth set in a light smile which showed a man of determination, and blue eyes which invited conversation but didn't seem to let you penetrate very far into the secrets concealed beneath his brow. I turned to the chapter where he described how the idea of taking an ox-hide boat across the Atlantic had first come into existence. I wanted to find out how he himself had seen the essence of his undertaking.

He had wanted above all to be certain that his idea had scientific value. He was also well aware that the whole project entailed a great deal of painstaking preparatory work. If he had gone to such efforts for the Brendan Voyage, I was sure that he would put no less effort into preparing the Jason Voyage and would research the subject thoroughly. So how could our expedition contribute to Tim Severin's expedition, apart from our theory about the gold ingot?

Questions like this were going through my mind, and I could hardly wait for ten o'clock to come, when I burst into Velizar Velkov's study.

'Yes, that's not a bad idea, meeting up with Tim Severin and exchanging the findings of the two expeditions,' Velkov agreed, 'as long as you have enough time to prepare your voyage. As far as our contribution is concerned, I'm sure that Severin will be interested in whatever we can offer: I'll put together a summary of what our submarine archaeologists have done so far. Misho Lazarov can contribute something about the stone anchors and early navigation in the Black Sea, and Zara Gocheva can add something about the Thracians and Asia Minor and the islands of the Aegean Sea in Apollonius Rhodius's *Argonautica*. I'll see if I can think of any other colleagues who might be able to help. And your job will be to find out exactly what new data Tim Severin's voyage aboard *Argo* has revealed, take a good look at his ship, bring back pictures of it, and find out how it was built. The most important thing now, though, is to find out about the schedule for Severin's expedition to Colchis. I think that I'll be able to help – I'll write to a good friend of mine, Othar Lordkipanidze. He's head of the Archaeology Centre of the Georgian Academy of Sciences and a leading specialist on Colchian history. If anyone knows anything about *Argo*'s arrival in Georgia, he will. It might be a good idea also to get in touch with Tim Severin beforehand so that he knows about our expedition and our eventual meeting, if we manage to get everything organised in time.'

After my meeting with the professor, I immediately got in touch with Theodora Davidova, who had translated Tim Severin's books into Bulgarian.

'The best thing would be to write to Hutchinson in London who publish his books,' she advised. 'They might be able to tell you where he is at the moment.'

The replies started coming in about a month later. Hutchinson informed me that Tim Severin was in the Mediterranean, and if I wished to send him a letter through them, they would try to forward it. I got something more definite from *Vokrug Sveta*. The chief editor, Alexander Poleshchuk himself, wrote to me, saying that he was interested in our expedition and would send the journalist Vitalii Babenko of the international department to meet us in Poti on 16–17 July. *Argo* was expected to arrive a few days later, on 18–19 July. Concerning Tim Severin's programme in Georgia itself, a special Jason Reception Committee had been set up, and we should get in touch with it to co-ordinate our meetings and work with Tim Severin.

Things had started moving. We already had specific dates, and had to get the preparation for our voyage over as quickly as possible. Sergei, who at such moments was an even greater optimist than myself, even considered the possibility of our sailing in the Aegean Sea, starting at the same place where *Argo* was being built at the moment.

'You forget,' I said, trying to rein him in a bit, 'that we don't even know yet where exactly *Argo* is being built. Nor do we know when she'll set sail, which yacht we will be using and how much spare time we'll have. And there wouldn't really be much point in sailing along with *Argo* all the time. The best thing would be for us to meet up somewhere in the Black Sea or at the finish in Georgia, so that we can exchange information between the two expeditions, as Professor Velkov recommends.'

Sergei agreed. He went to Moscow to co-ordinate our programme with Tim Severin's upon his arrival in Soviet waters.

At that time a letter from Dublin University arrived. Maurice Harmon said that he had seen Tim Severin a year previously, but hadn't heard from him since. He had now asked the editor of the *Irish Times* to help us, as that paper usually covered Severin's expeditions. They had sent him their latest interview with Severin, which had been taken by their photographer John Egan, who would also take part in the Jason Voyage.

In the photograph accompanying the interview, Tim Severin was standing smiling with a model of *Argo* in his hands, with the actual ship being built in the background. The caption beneath the picture said that *Argo* was being built on the Greek island of Spetses.

The interview also contained other interesting details: Severin's expedition would set off from Volos, the Argonauts' starting-point, at the beginning of May, with a crew of twenty who would row and sail all the way to Colchis. Half of this crew would stay on throughout the voyage. The other half would change: there would be Greek rowers in Greek waters, Turks in Turkey, and Georgians in Colchis. According to Severin, the Jason Voyage would resemble the Brendan Voyage in many ways. They would both be in open boats, they would both try to identify various points along the route, and both would be based on reliable sources: the Brendan Voyage on the ancient

TIM SEVERIN AND THE JASON VOYAGE

saga *Navigatio Sancti Brendani Abattis* and the Jason Voyage on *Argonautica* by Apollonius Rhodius.

Sergei brought good news back from Moscow. The organisers of *Argo*'s reception in Soviet waters had expressed interest in our expedition, and had confirmed the date of our expected arrival in Poti – 16–17 July. Apart from that, Tim Severin's main consultant on the Soviet side would be Velizar Velkov's friend, the Georgian archaeologist Othar Lordkipanidze, who was now expecting our expedition, too.

A few days later, more news came from Ireland. *Argo* had set sail from Spetses on her first trial run. In relatively calm spring weather, the ship had been rowed to Hydra, whence she would carry on to Volos, the ancient port of Iolcos, thus beginning the Jason Voyage.

4

THE SOUND OF ORPHEUS'S LYRE

> Starting with you, Phoebus, I shall mention the glorious deeds of the ancient heroes who, through the mouth of the Pontus and past the Cyanean Rocks on the orders of King Pelias, sailed the well-found *Argo* on their quest for the Golden Fleece . . .

With these words to Apollo Phoebus, god of the sun, music and poetical inspiration, and indeed of any outdoor activity, sailing included, Apollonius Rhodius begins his epic *Argonautica*. Tim Severin used it as his literary source for the Jason Voyage, and we used it for information about the Thracians in our expedition. What intrigued me was that in the very first verse of the poem, Apollonius says that he will 'mention', rather than give a detailed account of, the heroes who set off 'through the mouth of the Pontus', i.e. the Bosphorus, past the Cyanean or the Clashing Rocks which let no sailor through the Bosphorus. The Hellenic poet himself mentioned that others before him had extolled the ship built by Argus to the design of the goddess Athena. Thus, addressing the informed reader of his time, Apollonius found it unnecessary to dwell in any great detail on the pre-history of the quest for the Golden Fleece.

But this pre-history takes us back two generations before Jason, when Athamas had ruled the city of Orchomen in Boeotia, a region in central Greece. The son of Aeolus, god of the winds, he had had two children – Helle and Phrixus, daughter and son – through Nephele, goddess of the clouds. Ino, Athamas's second wife, felt hostile towards her two stepchildren, and so found a cunning way of dealing with them: she duped the women of Orchomen into drying their seeds, so that when they sowed them nothing grew. When Athamas sent messengers to the Delphic Oracle to find the reason for the infertility of their fields, Ino bribed the messengers into telling Athamas that Phrixus should be sacrificed to the gods, and that this would bring back the fertility of the fields and save the inhabitants of Orchomen from starvation.

Up to this point, there is nothing supernatural about the myth. It is a simple tale of palace intrigue, in which the queen and stepmother tries to get rid of the king's first-born son, the heir to the throne, and thus clear the way to the throne for her own son.

When the time comes for the sacrifice of Phrixus, the element of fantasy intervenes: the goddess Nephele sends a golden-fleeced ram to save her children. Phrixus and Helle mount it and ride off in a north-easterly direction. Even here, there is not necessarily anything fantastic about the whole story if we take the golden-fleeced ram, a gift from Hermes, the god of trade, to be simply a trading-ship specially prepared for the royal children's escape, a ship loaded with a cargo valuable enough to buy the favour of the foreign king with whom Phrixus and Helle would seek refuge. And these riches could have included a gold image of a ram, symbolising the fact that the royal house was of the Aeolian family since their emblem was a ram. And it is possible that later the Aeolids, heirs of Athamas and his brother Creteus, who was Jason's grandfather, took the ram as a symbol of royal power, of their unification, or of the salvation of their family, whose rightful heir had once stayed in Colchis; Phrixus had been brought up by Aeetes, king of the Colchians, who had married him off to his daughter Chalciopes, and had kept the Golden Fleece in the sacred forest belonging to the god of war, Ares. That was why the Greek heroes led by Jason knew that getting the Golden Fleece from Colchis was a tough assignment which they would not be able to fulfil by peaceful means.

But in order to come to Jason we have to go back to the Aeolian family, this time to Thessaly, in north-eastern Greece, on whose shores Creteus, brother of King Athamas, had built the city of Iolcos. Aeson, Creteus's son, succeeded him to the throne in the growing city. Power struggles seem to have been commonplace among the Aeolids – Pelias, brother of Aeson, overthrew him in a coup and Aeson was forced to live outside the city as a commoner. Aeson had just had a son, Jason, who would be the legitimate heir to the throne of Iolcos. Fearing an eventual attempt on the life of Jason by Pelias, Aeson announced that the child had died. But secretly he had taken him to Mount Pelion, where lived the wise centaur Chiron, who educated Jason. Jason lived there until he was twenty years old, when he decided to return to Iolcos and to take over from Pelias.

This is the point where Apollonius Rhodius begins his story in *Argonautica*. It had been foretold to Pelias that he was faced by death at the hands of a man who would arrive in Iolcos wearing only one sandal. On the way to Iolcos, Jason lost a sandal as he crossed the river Anavros. Pelias immediately saw the sign, and in order to put off the moment, he decided to make Jason, as claimant to the throne, sail to Colchis and bring back the Golden Fleece. Evidently at that time long voyages to strange lands and peoples were considered a convenient way of getting rid of somebody.

THE SOUND OF ORPHEUS'S LYRE

Making a brief mention of this reason for Jason's quest for the Golden Fleece, Apollonius quickly gets to the point of his tale and speaks about the families and names of the heroes, known as the Argonauts, or 'those sailing *Argo*', and then their actual voyage and their exploits on the way.

And here, right at the beginning of *Argonautica*, appeared the most prominent symbol of ancient Thrace, a name without which the heroes' feats were inconceivable – Orpheus. The Hellenic poet names him first in the list of the Argonauts.

> And so, let us first mention Orpheus who, it is said, was born of Calliope[1] herself, married to the Thracian Oyager, on Mount Pimpleus.[2] It is also said of him that with the sound of his songs he enchanted the hard rocks of the mountains and the waters of the streams. And the wild oaks which he enchanted with his lyre and led down from Pieria,[3] still grow thickly atop the high Thracian shore at Zone[4] which, like an incarnation of his music, stand close together in large numbers. This same Orpheus, who ruled Bistonian[5] Pieria, was accepted as his aide in his quests by Jason on the advice of Chiron.

Among the impressive list of 54 heroes, most of whom like Jason are Mycenaeans, we find the names of Hercules, the Dioscuran brothers Castor and Pollux, sons of Zeus, Peleus, the clairvoyant Idmon, and Lynceus, whose gaze was strong enough to penetrate rocks and mountains. Despite Pelius's

---

1 One of the nine muses, originally the goddess of song, and in the Hellenistic period the goddess of epic poetry.
2 A mountain range in Pieria.
3 A region in Thessaly between Olympus and the Bay of Salonika; and, with the same name, another region of the Lower Strouma valley in the Pangea mountains.
4 A Thracian town east of Maronea on the Aegean coast.
5 Bistonia has been identified as being near the mouth of the river Mesta.

objections, the Argonauts were also joined by his son Acastus, and Argus the ship-builder.

Apart from Orpheus, Apollonius Rhodius includes two other Thracians, whose background he describes in no less detail:

> Then came Zetes and Calais, sons of Boreas,[1] who were born of the daughter of Erechteus[2] of the Orethean dynasty on the rugged shores of Thrace, where the Thracian Boreas abducted her from Cecropea[3] while dancing by the Ilis[4] and, carrying her far away to the place of the Sarpedonian Rock,[5] he ravished her by the waters of the river Ergin,[6] enveloping her with dark clouds.

The ancient Greeks associated Boreas, the north wind, with Thrace because of the direction from which it blew. His daughters also have mythological connections with Thrace. Chiona was considered the mother of the mythical Thracian ruler Eumolpus, the originator of the Eleusian mysteries, who was also described as a renowned singer – his name meant 'he who sings delightfully' – and who was one of Orpheus's students and fellows. Boreas's other daughter, Cleopatra, was wife of the Thracian king Phineas. He too played an important role in their voyage, by helping them to get unharmed past the Symplegades, the rocks in the Bosphorus, after which Zetes and Calais rid him of the Harpies – half women, half birds – which kept stealing or fouling his food.

But while it is difficult to sort out what in Zetes and Calais are Thracian elements and what are just reflections of the Greek

1 God of the north wind.
2 A legendary Athenian king.
3 The original name of the Acropolis in Athens. It came from Cecrops, first mythical king of Athens.
4 A stream in Attica.
5 Cape Gremia, south of Enez.
6 Today the river Ergene.

view of the Thracians, the image of Orpheus, which has come to us in many different versions, is fundamentally Thracian in spirit. It contains elements of Thracian religion which were not characteristic of the Greeks: a belief in immortality, in reincarnation, in the divine nature of man, and in the state of bliss which man can achieve only through perfection of the spirit.

Throughout the spring months, as we were preparing the first stage of the Argonautica Expedition, amidst the confusion of rushing from pillar to post and trying to avoid the hidden rocks of modern-day red tape, which even the all-seeing Argonaut Lynceus would have had difficulty in dealing with, my most blissful moments, which gave me a sort of inner assurance that we would in the end reach Colchis, were my encounters with Orpheus. It was a real pleasure, late in the evenings, after a hard day's grappling with practical organisational problems, to engross myself in what ancient and modern scholars had written about the great Thracian bard. Some of them, such as Pausanius, treat Orpheus not as a mythological but as a historical figure: 'In my opinion Orpheus was a man who outmatched his predecessors with the beauty of his poems, and became highly influential as it was believed that he had discovered rites of the gods and ways of purifying impure deeds, as well as charms against sickness and the wrath of the gods.' Pausanius recounts various legends connected with Orpheus, and says: 'Anyone who has dealt with poetry knows that Orpheus's hymns are short and not very numerous ... In beauty they can be ranked second after the hymns of Homer, although they are above him in the blessing of the gods.' This in itself is great praise for the traditional culture of ancient Thrace, even though it was an oral rather than a written culture.

Others such as Cononus describe the death of Orpheus as if it were an actual event. After the death of Eurydice, Orpheus avoided women and banned them from attending his mysteries – these were secret rites, by means of which he reformed the Dionysian bacchanalia and orgies. Orpheus recommended that, in order to free the soul from the dark depths of the body, one had to lead a balanced earthly life – enlightenment, strict asceticism, no killing or eating the flesh of animals. When the men entered the shrine to carry out their sacred rites, they left their weapons outside the entrance. The women waited for a convenient moment, seized the weapons, attacked the Orpheans and cut Orpheus himself to pieces, throwing his dismembered body into the sea. According to Harrison, the British researcher of the Orphic rites, this is based on historical fact: possibly the Thracian women had fallen in a frenzy and attacked an outsider and prophet because they saw in his reforms a disregard for their traditional local rites.

It must have been common for people with new ideas to be put to death in those days – even in our own times such individuals can be unpopular, although they do not necessarily have to forfeit their lives. What I found interesting was how Orpheus's name had survived through the ages, and how his fame had grown to the extent that even the ancient Greeks had included him on the voyage of the Argonauts. The earliest mention of Orpheus we have today is that by the poet Ibices, who described him as the 'glorious renowned Orpheus'. Other poets of the sixth century BC described Orpheus as the son of Apollo, god of the sun, associating him with the Thracian sun-cult, which lies at the basis of the Orphic cult. In the third century BC Apollonius Rhodius put him first in the list of the Argonauts, not omitting to mention his Thracian origins; as well as mentioning his qualities as a bard, he also ascribes to him those of pacifier and wise man. It is Orpheus who settles the first dispute among the Argonauts, which takes place before they have even set sail from Iolcos, by singing a song about the creation of the world:

THE SOUND OF ORPHEUS'S LYRE

And Orpheus, raising his lyre[1] in his left hand, started singing. He sang of how the earth, the sky and the sea, initially bound together in a single entity, were separated after a vicious struggle among themselves; how the stars, the moon and the paths of the sun always take their particular place in the sky; how the mountains rose and the rushing streams were created together with the nymphs and with all living creatures. He finished, sustaining a long note with his lyre and his divine voice. And even after he had stopped, they still sat there, their necks craning forward, listening, completely still in their delight; so strongly had the spell of the song entered them.

At the time when Apollonius wrote his *Argonautica*, Orphism, or the system of rites and beliefs whose origins were ascribed to Orpheus, had spread from Thrace to Hellas, southern Italy and Sicily, and had many adherents. Orpheus was already a figure depicted in art, most often as a man holding a lyre. An example is the famous painting on an Attic crater[2] of the fifth century BC, where he is shown sitting on a rock playing to Thracians wearing their typical Thracian dress. But another image of Orpheus sticks in my mind – the one I had seen in Delphi on an item of the Sycionian treasure – where he is shown standing upright aboard *Argo*. This treasure also pre-dates Apollonius Rhodius – it is from the sixth century BC – and so the Hellenic poet might well have been inspired by this image of the Thracian bard when he described him as 'raising his lyre in his left hand' before the Argonauts.

'If Orphism was at its height at the time of Apollonius,' Zara Gocheva told me at one of our consultations about *Argonautica*, 'it's likely that the image of Orpheus came into the epic of the Argonauts precisely during the Hellenic period. As far as we

---

1 In the original this is a phorminx, the earliest Greek stringed instrument, and a version of the lyre.
2 A kind of ancient pottery vessel.

can tell from the records that have come down to us, Apollonius Rhodius is the first to mention Orpheus as an Argonaut. There might have been a Thracian priest, who may or may not have been called Orpheus, in the original Thessalonian–Boeotian epic cycle. In the Late Bronze Age, the time of the Argonauts, we can already speak of Thracians proper; that was when the earliest Greek authors, in particular Homer, used the name Traice or Treice to designate the lands north of Greece, with which they had comparatively few dealings.'

'The main thing,' I said, 'is that in Apollonius's *Argonautica* Orpheus is definitely associated with Thrace. I even noticed that he's given much more mention in the first and second songs, when *Argo* is sailing past Thrace.'

'That's right. I think that the episode on the island of Samothrace is especially indicative, when Orpheus invites the heroes to take part in the local mystery rites. And the great Samothracian gods, the Cabiri, are often associated with him, which is why Orpheus guides the Argonauts to them for eventual assistance on their voyage. This tells us that navigation must have been quite developed among the local Thracians if they worshipped them. And this cult later spread along the Thracian coast of the Black Sea, too.'

'Have any other historians dealt with the links between Orpheus and *Argonautica*, and with sailing in general?'

Zara Gocheva thought for a while.

'I don't remember anyone dealing particularly with that theme. Some colleagues of mine, such as Professor Fol, mention in passing that Orpheus was associated with water – maybe that'll help you a little . . .'

When I tried to find Professor Alexander Fol, who is head of the Thracian Studies Institute and one of the most prominent researchers of ancient Thracian culture, it turned out that he was in Delphi. I learned later that he had been there inspecting various shrines, tombs and sacrificial altars cut into the rocks, which led him to conclude that Delphi itself had been a vast rock shrine to the Thraco-Pelasgean culture after the middle of the second millennium BC – which was another link, a temporal one in this case, between Thracian Orphism and the age of the Argonauts.

One of Professor Fol's assistants from the Institute, Valery Roussinov, updated me on the professor's latest findings:

'Thracian Orphism was a highly complex teaching about the origins of the world, the formation of society and the road to human self-perfection. The main figure behind it all was the mythical and real king (priest, bard and teacher) who was known under different names – Orpheus, Zalmoxis, Resus, Tamiris, Phineas, etc. The king bound himself to the forces of nature by a mystical marriage to Mother Earth, thus acquiring superhuman forces and the ability to see into the future and to subjugate his people. After his death he became a human deity, merging with the sun, while the urn containing his ashes was kept in rock niches, caves and dolmens, all of them symbolising the womb of Mother Earth. In Thracian society, where there was no writing and there was only an oral tradition, this mythical story was kept secret and only told to the small circle of those "initiated" into the teaching, by stories, acting and a system of rituals.'

'But why did the Hellenes find it necessary to include this particular Thracian priest-king in the epic of the Argonauts?' I asked.

'Orpheus takes part in the quest of the Argonauts for the Golden Fleece which guarantees Hellenic might. It's probably an expression of the active involvement of Thracian values in the synthesis which led to the rise of Hellenic culture.'

I asked Valery about what Zara Gocheva had told me – the

connection between Orpheus and water. He rummaged around in the Institute library and came out with a manuscript. In the manuscript, Professor Fol had the following to say on the matter:

Orpheus is undoubtedly a chthonic symbol. The water (chthonic) element constantly accompanies the soothsayer. Orpheus travels aboard *Argo*. Euridyce is bitten by a snake beside a stream. He twice crosses the Styx in the form of a swan, and his head is thrown into a river. Atop his lyre, his head floats across the sea to Lesbos. There is already a hypothesis that Orpheus was a water-deity, either a swan or a bard, which is in fact the same thing, as with the mythical Cuecnos, who turns into a swan. Orpheus's transformation into a swan appears quite late in literature, at the end of the fifth century. The swan is a symbol of music. The death of Orpheus is related to the swan-song. Another idea is that Cuecnos, which is the name of a marine fish which hides among the rocks, should be interpreted to mean a sacred fish, which is an attribute of Mithridates, a god who is another incarnation of Orpheus.

The search for other possible links between Orpheus and the Argonauts and their quest for the Golden Fleece took me also to a man who was investigating ancient pre-Christian elements in Bulgarian folklore, Professor Ivan Venedikov. He was working on a book entitled *The Golden Pillar of the Proto-Bulgarians*, and, as it happened, when I met him he was just working on ancient legends and epics with parallels in Bulgarian folksongs. With his characteristic eloquence, he started telling me about the golden apples of Bulgarian folklore and the Golden Fleece, about the *Orphic Argonautica* and the dragon guarding the strange mythological tree, the sleeping wood-nymphs by the tree with the golden apples... I listened to this white-haired old man in a trance, not daring to interrupt him with my questions, the way people must have once listened to the tales of an old wise man. At one stage it occurred to me that the Golden Fleece which I had set out to find on the other side of the sea was right here beside me, in the form of the wealth of information I was obtaining by meeting people like this.

'In ancient times, young men went to pick golden apples, and of course the fruit of other trees, too,' Professor Venedikov began, as if telling a fairy-tale. 'The legend of the hero who goes to kill a serpent which guards a tree can be found among most peoples. And in our part of the world a similar hero was known in ancient times. We can see him on many Thracian relief carvings dedicated to an anonymous household god, whom the Thracians simply called Cheroi, or "hero-god", and whom they represented as a horseman brandishing a lance and carrying a shield. The depiction of the Thracian god as a heroic horseman is very important to us, as it shows that there was a widespread legend about a young-man-turned-god which was quite clearly connected with a tree and a serpent winding around it, in front of an altar guarded by one or several women. Such legends, it seems, were common among all peoples living around the Black Sea in ancient times. The legend of the Golden Fleece is one of these. It is given in Apollonius Rhodius's *Argonautica*, but is also known in different versions by later authors. A more Thracian version of this legend was recorded in the late Roman era and ascribed to the old Thracian bard Orpheus who had told of the adventures of the Argonauts after accompanying them on their journey.'

As Professor Venedikov pulled out sheaves of paper from beneath the thick tomes on his desk, I recalled hearing about the *Orphic Argonautica*. Written in about the third or fourth century AD, it was an epic poem of 1,376 verses about Orpheus's participation in the Argonauts' voyage. In this version, he played the roles of the priests and soothsayers Mopsus and Idmon, presided over the purification rites and sacrifices, and demonstrated the magical powers of his art by drowning out the fatal songs of the Sirens and making the Clashing Rocks or Symplegades stand still at the 'mouth of the Pontus' so that *Argo* could pass them safely.

'In this poem,' Professor Venedikov went on, 'the credit for lulling the dragon to sleep is ascribed to Orpheus's magical songs as well as to the spells of Medea. The tale of the voyage and the theft of the Golden Fleece is told by Orpheus himself. Orpheus's and Medea's magical songs make all the goddesses of the underworld go to sleep. In this way they open the gates of the fortress in which the Golden Fleece is kept, and, before the Argonauts' very eyes, the forest itself appears.'

Professor Venedikov took one of the sheets of paper he had pulled out, and, in the monotone voice of an ancient rhapsodus[1] read some verses from the *Orphic Argonautica*. Then he fell silent, engrossed in what he had read, and finally raised his head.

'This is how a later poet, from about the time of the adoption of Christianity, pictured the taking of the Golden Fleece. In fact, the Golden Fleece is a symbol of the wealth guarded by the dragon and by all goddesses of the underworld. And again, the altar of Zeus is attended by women, as we see in the bas-reliefs depicting the Thracian hero.'

'And what is the connection between that and the Bulgarian folk epic?'

This seemed to be the cue Professor Venedikov had been waiting for. He inundated me in a flood of examples of Bulgarian epic songs with parallels in mythology – about young men who have to cross the Black Sea to bring back the Golden

---

[1] One of the itinerant singers in Greece who told epic poems to the accompaniment of the lyre.

THE SOUND OF ORPHEUS'S LYRE

Apples from there – a considerable exploit. There is also the dragon, and there are wood-nymphs, who are the equivalent of the goddesses who guard the Golden Fleece.

After Professor Venedikov and the world of the *Orphic Argonautica* and the folk epic, I moved on to the world of the mystic Orphic rites, or Orphic mysteries, and their links with archaic secret societies, which were described to me in no less gripping a manner by Ivan Marazov, another scholar working on Thracian mythology and culture. I was struck by the difference in style between the two, putting it down to the influence of their subjects. While Venedikov had sounded to me like an old-time story-teller whose knowledge came from somewhere deep down in the roots, in the earth, in folk tradition, Marazov, who was at that moment working on 'aristocratic mystic societies', seemed to get the power of his imagination from sources which were only available to the select few. He based his work on the idea that the Orphic doctrine was propagated as an ideology only to those initiated into the mystery rites. He discounted as historically inaccurate the claims of many classical authors that the Thracians all believed in immortality. Professor Marazov had enough evidence to demonstrate a similarity between the Thracian mysteries and the archaic secret societies, which could be joined only after certain selection procedures. For example, women were banned from the Orphic mysteries, and the rites organised by the Thracian bard were open only to married warriors.

'We can see this from the reason for Orpheus's murder,' the professor said. 'Because he "involved the men in wanderings" and not the women, thus making them jealous, and also from the ritual before entering the mystery hall, when the men had to leave their arms outside the door. In archaic society, this was evidently the warrior-class, which included the entire aristocracy. Thus the Orphic mysteries were open only to members of the aristocratic warrior-class.'

'Perhaps that was also what the Hellenic poets implied by putting Orpheus among the other heroes of *Argo*, who were all members of the aristocratic warrior-class,' I proposed. 'Actually, I've always wondered what other reason there could be for including Orpheus on a major expedition of this kind. Could travel in general have been an element of the Orphic doctrine?'

I hadn't expected Professor Marazov to agree with my guess, but he nodded:

'The ritual practices of aristocratic mystic societies probably included travel in some form. Perhaps its mythological prototype was the "wanderings" of the Thracians, led by Orpheus. Such travel could have taken different forms, such as an ascent to a mountain peak, for example, or a pilgrimage to different sacred shrines . . .'

Professor Marazov started rummaging about in his books and brought out one bound in black leather. He continued:

'This is what Erastotenes of Alexandria, a contemporary of Apollonius, says: "He [Orpheus] . . . considered Helius to be the greatest of the gods, whom he also called Apollo. And rising early one morning and climbing to the top of the mountain of Pangea, he waited there for the sun to rise, so that he might be the first to see it." This climb is a kind of ritual journey to profess his belief in the cult of the sun, to an Orphic shrine. And travelling to different sacred places can be taken to mean the visits of the kings of the Getae and Tribali tribes to the lands of the Odrisae, which can be seen from inscriptions on pottery from northern Thrace. So, before you set off for Colchis, you might do well to take an Orphic trip around the Rhodopes, and pray to Apollo to protect you on your voyage,' he smiled.

He hardly suspected that that was just what I was intending

to do. Not to pray to Apollo or beg his protection on some mountain summit, but to meet a man who had been described to me as the modern incarnation of an Orphic poet. Until then I had only heard of Nikola Gigov from his poems and his marvellous essays about the Rhodopes, or Rhodope, as he liked to call the mountain range, using the feminine version of the name. As we were planning the Argonautica Expedition, several articles had appeared in the magazine *Echo* by Nikola Gigov, revealing his other big love, apart from Rhodope, which was Orpheus. His main theory was that, before becoming a mythical figure, Orpheus had been a real-life singer from the Rhodopes.

The articles had excited a great deal of reader interest, and many opinions and further questions had come in. Nikola Gigov had obviously challenged the academic world with his attempts to bridge the gap between Orpheus and the folklore of the Rhodopes. So when in spring I wrote to the *Echo* office asking them if they could assist in any way on the forthcoming Argonautica Expedition, they suggested that we first undertake a symbolic journey to Orpheus in the Rhodopes with Nikola Gigov. The magazine *Discover Bulgaria*, on which I worked as an editor, joined the effort. And so I went to Smolyan, the town where Nikola Gigov lived. Amidst the confusion of preparations for the sea expedition to Colchis, this trip to the Rhodopes remains one of my most pleasant memories of the pre-expedition months.

There were four of us – Nikola Gigov, the magazine photographer Todor Mitov, my father Ivan, who caught the travel bug from me from time to time and would join me in the mountains, and myself. As soon as we set out on our hike, a deer crossed our path.

'The ancients took that as a good omen!' Nikola smiled.

'It would have been an even better one if I'd had a rifle on me. Then we'd have seen how well it goes with Ivan's white wine!' said Todor, shaking his head sadly and giving my father a slap on the shoulder with his heavy paw.

'You know, Todor reminds me of a satyr in the suite of Dionysus,' said Nikola. 'Thick-set, muscular, fond of eating and drinking – all he needs is a bushy beard.'

'I don't need any beard, but just let me come across a Bacchante, I'll show her some mystic rites!' Todor grinned, rubbing his hands together. 'I'm a down-to-earth type. You and Theodor go off chasing Orpheuses around the peaks – he's a bit up in the clouds too, you'll get on well together!'

This division of the group into Dionysians and Orpheans proved quite fruitful for our journey back to the time when, according to Nikola, Orpheus had walked the mountains. Todor, like any photographer, wanted to see everything Nikola told him about with his own eyes. He stubbornly refused to see the connection between anything and Orpheus. To him Orpheus's flower was just a 'clump of weeds', and the ruins of an ancient building in a place known as Orphensko were 'a couple of old stones'. His distrustful questions forced Nikola to delve deep into the stores of his knowledge in a wide variety of directions. Near the village of Gela, for example, Nikola started rushing around over the meadows until he came across a whole colony of small white bell-shaped flowers with a pale purple colour near some rocks.

'That's it!' he cried. 'Orpheus's flower! Its botanical name is *Haberlea rhodopensis*, and it was discovered in the first half of the nineteenth century by an expedition. People call it by different names in different places. Here they call it *shap*,[1] for example. It is depicted on an ancient coin in the Plovdiv Archaeological Museum. Rhodope, in the form of a young

---

1 *Shap* – Bulgarian for foot-and-mouth disease.

woman, holds the flower as a symbol of the mountains' mystery and majesty. There is also another coin showing Orpheus sitting on a rock playing the lyre surrounded by wild animals and birds.'

'I still don't see the connection between the flower and Orpheus,' grumbled Todor as he rolled around in the grass to find a good vantage-point from which to photograph it. 'If it's called *shap*, it must have something to do with sheep.'

'You're right there,' smiled Nikola. 'On St George's Day the people crush it and put it into the sheep's fodder to prevent foot-and-mouth disease. But in ancient times the flower was called *citara*, which Pseudoplutarchus explains as follows: when the Bacchantes tore Orpheus to pieces, where his blood had spilt, this flower, called citara, grew, and whenever the Dionysian festivals were celebrated, it gave out the sound of a guitar.'

'Oh, so it's a guitar now, is it? That pseudo-what's-his-name guy must have been hearing things,' Todor muttered as he focused his camera, while Nikola laughed good-naturedly and continued with his arguments:

'The two main elements of the Orphic doctrine are reincarnation and immortality. And Orpheus's flower is a symbol of precisely that. What makes it rare is that it can fall into a state of anabiosis, or apparent death. Botanists have tried keeping a plucked specimen in a herbarium for two years, and then planted it back in its natural environment, where it thrived again. Apart from that, some scholars believe that the lost works of Orpheus included one on natural and magical botany, which could have been about the medical properties of the herbs of the Rhodopes. It wouldn't be surprising if Orpheus had known about anabiosis, hypnosis and other secrets of the mind. There is another theory that he was the first renowned healer in Thracian folk medicine.'

'Ah, so that's why the Argonauts took him with them!' Todor immediately concluded with his practical mind. 'Not because they wanted to listen to his music, but because they wanted him to be their doctor!'

'His medical activities were not just confined to herbal remedies,' Nikola went on, trying to ignore him. 'But also to music and words, which work on the mind rather than the body. If you like, we could go into Gela now and I'll introduce you to Manol Trendafilov. To me he is the memory of folk-healers incarnate.'

Half an hour later, the wizened old shepherd from Gela was reciting a strange incantation, first in a monotone and then melodically, to the serpent in an unknown language. I managed to catch only the odd combination of words, as the old man could only recite his incantations like tongue-twisters, which was how it had been taught to him by his father and his father's father.

'In my opinion,' Nikola said, 'such incantations, which are also used during herbal treatment, are a kind of magic spell, which is a purely Orphic element in Rhodope. What interests me is not the degree to which these incantations might be superstitious and to what extent they are medical, but the actual words they contain, which to my mind are remnants of the ancient Thracian language.'

Nikola took us to many other places – the Ardino basin, the Trigrad Gorge region, Dospat and Lyubcha, where in a spot known as Orphensko he showed us the remains of stone-paved roads and an ancient building, and took us to meet old people from the village, who told us that according to their fathers, Orphensko had once been the site of a city, where 'someone called Orpheus' had lived. 'He was the first singer ... And not just a singer, he was also the king ...'

On the last day of our journey we were sitting on Orpheus's

rocks enjoying the view over the Smolyan lakes. I asked Nikola what had first got him interested in Orpheus.

'Orpheus became part of my life together with the songs of the Rhodopes, and I've been studying him ever since. Even in my university dissertation on *Poetry and Rhodope*, and now with the anthology of songs from the Rhodopes I'm preparing with two other researchers, I have become increasingly convinced that the deepest roots of the songs of the Rhodopes go back to Orpheus. My goal might be modest, but to me it's important: to get as far back to the roots of our folklore and Rhodope's fame as the home of Orpheus so that I can start asking questions. After all, I'm a poet, and asking questions is my job. But I hope that there'll be scholars able to answer them for me.'

Todor came away from the Rhodopes rather disappointed. Maybe he had hoped right until the last moment that Nikola Gigov would finally reveal to us some sacred shrine containing the skull of Orpheus. I came away with far more questions than I had set out with. One idea that kept going through my mind more and more frequently was one suggested by the writer Plamen Tsonev, who had given me his book *Orpheus the Soothsayer* a few days before my trip to the Rhodopes:

> Archaeologists recently discovered another shrine to the sun-god Helios or Apollo, the mythological father of Orpheus, the leader of the muses. This discovery made me wonder what the result would be if, instead of a temple to the sun-god, the archaeologists had discovered the tomb of Orpheus (whose existence is confirmed by Diodorus and Pausanius, the latter saying that it existed right until the second century AD), and if the honour of announcing the discovery had fallen to me. What a sensation that would have been all over the world! And I realised that our civilised world would really be much more excited if Orpheus's seventh vertebra, little finger or tibia had been found than if all his art and poetry and his entire psychology had been restored.

So I started wondering why some people today would be far more interested in touching a skull, rather than experiencing the spiritual world of a great man.

Plamen Tsonev had also given me one of his studies of Orpheus, asking me to give it to Tim Severin when we met. Throughout my quest for Orpheus – both during my talks with the scholars and during my wanderings in the Rhodopes, I felt that when we sailed *Argo* we should take something more with our expedition than just a pile of articles; we should take with us a symbol of the intellectual power of the Thracian bard and Argonaut. It was the search for such a symbol that took me to my home town Plovdiv, where I visited the wood-carver Rangel Stoilov. I remembered that in his latest exhibition of small wooden sculpture I had noticed his tendency to base himself on the earliest mythological and folkloric traditions, and to seek universal values in them. That was just what I needed if I wanted a work of art expressing the idea of Orpheus.

I didn't need to make any lengthy explanations to Rangel.

'None of my works has been at sea yet, or taken part in an expedition!' he said, stroking his bushy beard. Suddenly he asked: 'And what is Severin's boat made out of?'

'Wood, of course. They haven't even used nails, which is how the original *Argo* was made.'

'I see. So I suppose he'll know good wood when he sees it. Right. In that case, I'll use lime.'

Then he started sketching something and seemed to forget my presence. After some time, he raised his head and said:

'Come back one week before you set sail. There isn't much time, but we'll get Orpheus to life by then.'

At about the same time I met the artist Mikhail Peshev in the *Echo* office. He was a great enthusiast for all kinds of novel undertakings to do with the mysteries of ancient civilisations, and since he had been highly intrigued by the Argonautica Expedition he offered to design an emblem for us. Free of charge, just like Rangel!

'One can be an Argonaut but once in one's life, even if it's only indirectly!' said Mikhail excitedly.

Ten days later I found a large unstamped envelope in my letter-box, delivered by hand. Inside there was a large piece of card with a stylistic emblem for the Argonautica Expedition, and a note which read as follows:

> I am deeply convinced that the legends of the ancient world are the key to understanding the modern world. For each legend is like a sound vessel in which, going back in time, one actually moves forward by understanding the eternal truths about things.
>
> Today the legendary ship of the Argonauts exists no more. But it exists as a symbol of the questing human spirit, ever striving for new worlds. As an artist I have tried to find my own key to the legend, and I will be happy if this lives up to the expectations of those of you who will now travel in time. I have depicted the ship in bold, moving lines of light and dark, alternating them in the way that night and day alternate in a human life. There are eight of one and nine of the other, for the ancients symbolised success with the figure nine, and the diplomacy and skill it took to reap that success with the figure eight. The mast of the ship is in fact Orpheus's harp, i.e. the support which catches the wind of expectation and hope in a successful outcome. And, taken together, the ship with mast and sails looks like a pen, which symbolises the art which the voyage itself and its description will be. All this is surrounded by a square, which symbolises the completeness of the expedition.

Mikhail Peshev's gesture made me realise how very much the legend of the Argonauts and of Orpheus is still alive nowadays, as long as one has a sense of history and doesn't live just within the confines of one's life-span, looking neither forward nor backward.

Rangel had approached his work with a similar idea of the link between the worldly and the cosmic in human life. When I visited his studio for a second time, I saw a wooden figure which glowed warmly with the symbolism which the sculptor had evoked in it. Its deep symbolism immediately caught the imagination. I could hardly have described it better than the sculptor himself:

'To my mind, Orpheus is the tremor of the music of the cosmos on earth which legends tell us of. It's like an aerial, a transmitter between the universe and the earth. The lyre is like raised hands plucking the strings and, like antennae, sensing the music of the universe. And the antennae also come from deep down in the ground, because the two feet are in fact trunks which are firmly rooted. From them comes a floral ornament which climbs up like an umbilical cord, branching out into hands which are held over the strings, receiving the cosmic music which fertilises the things that are of this world. That's what Orpheus was aboard *Argo*: a Thracian priest, an intermediary between the Heavens and the Earth.'

And so the Thracian Argonaut was ready to accompany us to Colchis, and the Argonautica emblem was also ready to decorate the decks of our yacht.

At that moment, Tim Severin's *Argo* had already set sail from Volos on the Jason Voyage, and was sailing almost in the same way as Apollonius had described in *Argonautica* – albeit without the sound of Orpheus's music:

> ... and to the sound of Orpheus's music their oars struck the turbulent waters of the sea, while the roaring waves broke on the surface and the foaming black sea-water churned about, seething under the energy of those strong men ...

5

THE CREW

All these years, and even now at sea, it has seemed to me that the real problem is not so much building the craft as finding a crew suitable for long expeditions, a crew in which each member is not only a good sailor, but also an expert in his field, be he cameraman, maritime historian, journalist or whatever. And, apart from that, they have to be good friends and know their place in the team; because when more than three Bulgarians get together you find at least nine different opinions on each question. What I'd like – although I can't imagine it really happening – is for us to get together a team like the one Tim Severin had on the Brendan Voyage.

These had been Stoicho's words, and they came back to me when I had to start giving some serious thought to the question of the future crew of the Argonautica Expedition. Stoicho Stoichev, known to his friends as 'Roissa', was the man who had first given me the travel bug so long ago. A diver, pot-holer, mountaineer, yachtsman and by profession a journalist, he had climbed innumerable mountain peaks in Europe, Africa and Asia; he had crossed the Sahara several times, and sailed in the Black, Baltic and Mediterranean seas. As head of the Travellers' Club in Plovdiv, which was where he had first fired my interest in travel, Roissa's latest undertaking had been a sailing expedition in several stages on a cruiser built by the members of the club.

It was on one of the first voyages aboard this yacht when Roissa had told me his views on getting the crew together for an expedition. He had just read Tim Severin's *The Brendan Voyage* and it had made a deep impression on him. That was the reason for his categorical view:

'Tim Severin is just my idea of a modern traveller. I don't believe that anyone can get together a team like he did.'

One year after this conversation, when I had to get together the crew for the Argonautica Expedition, Roissa was no longer among us to advise me. He had died of a heart attack aboard a yacht during a storm off Istanbul. So, remembering his words about the crew of *Brendan*, I again leafed through Severin's book. I wanted to see how the British traveller's crew members had got into his team.

I learned that only the first crew-member, George Mallone, had been previously personally known to Tim – they had sailed the Mediterranean together in a small craft, and Tim considered him to be an unsurpassed yachtsman. The next crew-member, the Irishman Arthur Magan, had got in touch with Severin through George while they were still constructing the *Brendan*. He described himself in a letter to Tim as having sailed ever since he was old enough to walk around a boat. Then Peter Mullett, a former photo-reporter who had moved to Ireland, appeared on the scene. He arrived carrying a big suitcase with a partition in it; one half contained photographic equipment, and the other contained a set of well-used carpenter's tools. Last of all came the Norwegian Rolf Hansen, who was a fanatical devotee of old boats. His favourite hobby was talking to old fishermen of distant villages on the Norwegian coast and collecting memories and tales of the times when people used to fish in sailing ships. If people asked him whether he was married, Rolf would reply, 'To the sea.'

During the Brendan Voyage itself, new people would join to replace those who had to leave for one reason or another. But there was never any friction between these men, who had not even known each other before, even though they were confined to a miniature craft made of hide, spending two seasons sailing among the storms and ice of the most merciless regions of the Atlantic.

So what was the solution? On the one hand, Roissa admired *Brendan*'s motley crew, while, on the other, he had, ever since the foundation of the club, been trying to do exactly the opposite, as he had told me then aboard the yacht:

'Instead of getting together a crew of individuals who don't know each other, each one with his own fixed ways and habits, I've tried to get them together during my fifteen years in the club. But whether these people will remain together on longer future voyages, or how my experiment will turn out, I have no idea.'

Torn between Roissa's experience and what I had read in Tim Severin's book, I finally decided to compromise: I resolved that the best thing would be for the Argonautica Expedition to consist partly of people whom I knew well, and partly of people sought from elsewhere; however, my main criteria for selection would be their yachting experience and their reasons for wanting to take part in the expedition.

Who did we have so far?

Obviously the first nominee would have to be Sergei – we had dreamed of this expedition together, and had planned it together for the UNESCO Scientific Expeditions Club (of which Sergei was vice-chairman at the time). So we would both be sailing to Colchis. Apart from all else, he was also a yachtsman. On the Malta expedition the captain kept him at the helm as much as possible: the reason was to keep him busy navigating; otherwise he would spend hours fiddling with various gadgetsand cluttering up the place so much that we would have to tread carefully in the cockpit, the galley and even in our bunks.

Another member of the crew would be Mikhail Lazarov. Like the stone anchors he was so fond of studying, he himself would act as a stabilising anchor to hold Sergei and myself back when we started getting carried away with our theories and hypotheses.

Then we would need somebody from the UNESCO Scientific Expeditions Club who was an experienced yachtsman, and who would also have contacts in the main Bulgarian yacht clubs in Varna and Bourgas to get them to help the expedition along. We needed a cruising yacht with about seven or eight berths suitable for a long cruise and presentable enough so that we could fly the Bulgarian flag from it when we met Tim Severin's international crew.

In the UNESCO Scientific Expeditions Club, we had not organised an expedition on such a scale in conjunction with either of the yacht clubs, and Sergei and I spent a long time wondering who to burden with the delicate task of mediator. But we would only know that we needed a yacht when we were sure the expedition would actually take place. And we wouldn't need just a yacht, but also a suitable crew and skipper who would also have to be enthusiastic about the expedition.

One evening as Sergei and I were hatching plans at our home, my wife Maria mentioned that in a couple of days she would be taking part in a regatta in Varna. Sergei slapped his forehead and looked at me.

'Where the hell have we been all this time? Here we are, wondering who to send around the marinas, and Maria here is off there whilst we're sitting around wondering!'

THE CREW

'But Apollonius Rhodius didn't say anything about there being women among the Argonauts...'

'Just forget about Apollonius Rhodius, will you!' said Sergei vehemently. 'Tomorrow I'll bring you my *Oxford Maritime Dictionary* and show you where it says that in one version of the story one of the Argonauts, Atlanta, was disguised as a man...'

So we decided to give it a try, and see if Maria could use her powers of persuasion on one of Varna's yacht captains. Maria Yoreva, or 'Yorrie', as she was known in yachting circles, was a seasoned yachting and wind-surfing competitor, and knew all of the more experienced yachtsmen. As well as that, she had been on long-distance cruises with all-male crews. She had also been on the previous year's expedition to Malta, where we had got married, having previously started work together on a book entitled *Travel, That Incurable Bug*. Yorrie, like me, was a journalist and her participation in the expedition might rally the support of the Sofia daily *Otechestven Vestnik*, on which she edited a column entitled, 'Cor Caroli'.

One week later, Yorrie came back from Varna and announced: 'We'll be sailing aboard the yacht *Aurora* with Henro. He'll choose a couple of other yachtsmen and talk to his bosses. We've got to get off an official letter as soon as possible.'

I knew Henrich Kokonchev by name rather than personally. Rated a Master of Sport in yachtsmanship, he had recently undertaken the first long-distance winter yachting cruise in the Black Sea together with another famous yachtsman from Varna, Dimiter Genchev. At the moment he was a captain in the Varna Transport Company's marine tourism department, and skipper of *Aurora*, a two-master mahogany yacht of the Conrad 45 class, built in Poland. She would be an excellent way of getting to Colchis.

I immediately sorted out official proposals from the

THE ARGONAUTICA EXPEDITION

UNESCO Scientific Expeditions Club on a joint expedition, and set off for Varna. I was received by Henro. He was a man of about thirty-five to forty, although his hair was showing signs of going grey, with a healthy athletic physique, and he had a one-sided smile which seemed to say: 'What you've set out to do might succeed, but, then again, it mightn't – let's see what Fate holds in store for you . . .' At the same time his constantly squinting eyes and his tightly locked brows implied the character of a man who would relentlessly pursue his goal once he had decided on it.

The yachtsmen whom Henro had chosen were waiting to meet us at the Transport Company's bar called the Golden Wheel.

'I never thought that our quest for the Golden Fleece went via the Golden Wheel!' Misho remarked. He had come out of sheer curiosity, in order to see for himself who our skipper would be, and what kind of crew he had chosen for us.

'Stoyan Hristov and Peter Kaloyanov,' Henro said, introducing the 'boys', who had the same fit, athletic figures as he, although they were younger, as indeed they should be, but old enough to be staid and experienced, both in life and at sea.

Stoyan turned out to be a taxi-driver. He had got his driving licence at the age of seventeen, and been a rally driver for a short while, until he had decided to 'take it easy' and choose a safer – or so his wife thought – career as a yachtsman. We soon found out that his love of high speeds certainly hadn't been dampened when he had quit motor-racing. Whenever he was afloat, Stoyan was constantly wondering which sail to hoist to give the yacht a little more 'juice'. He was always under the impression that we were moving too slowly – if given the chance, he'd have rigged up his handkerchief to use as a sail.

Peter (Petyo) would distinguish himself as an excellent yachtsman, and was much more staid than Stoyan was. He preferred to weigh up the overall situation and not hoist more sails than were required for us to progress at a safe and easy pace. As the former head of an emergency group at the Devnya Chemical Works, he was obviously one unused to asking for trouble, and preferred to lay the groundwork carefully. Whenever he saw something out of its proper place on the yacht, especially if Sergei had just passed that way before him, he'd say: 'At sea, as well as on land, nothing is too small to be ignored!'

At that preliminary conversation in the Golden Wheel, Petyo surprised me by solving another problem that had long been on my mind – who the expedition photographer would be. Both Sergei and I were amateur photographers, but that wouldn't be enough, and, anyway, we would be too occupied to be full-time photographers. It turned out that Petyo was also an 'amateur photographer', but one with three independent exhibitions to his name! When he started reeling off a list of the equipment he'd take with him and what types of film he'd need to make a complete record of the expedition, I felt another weight off my shoulders. Misho Lazarov was also happy at the prospect of our obtaining good photographs of the archaeological sites we were going to visit – something which he considered very important.

However, the most important thing of all at that initial talk with the Varna crew was to see which way the captain's smile would go. Henro had so far taken part only in races, whose purpose is entirely different from that of expeditions. So I was eager to hear what he thought of our idea.

'Bulgarian yachtsmen don't know the route from Bulgaria along the coast of Asia Minor and to Georgia very well yet. From my own point of view both the route and the weather patterns in the region are interesting, as they will be of help on future expeditions to Georgia. It'll also be interesting for me personally because I haven't sailed that route before.' Henro withdrew his hand from his beard and started counting on his fingers. 'That was number one. The other thing that attracts me is the opportunity of meeting Tim Severin. The records of his previous voyages are interesting from a maritime point of view. I don't think there has been anyone in recent years to rival him in the kind of voyages he has undertaken. That's the second reason,' said Henro, bending back another finger. 'It'll also be interesting sailing with a mixed crew. For me this will be the first experiment combining a crew of yachtsmen proper, who will concentrate on the sailing, and a team of scientists who will be occupied with their studies. And it'll also be my first voyage with a woman on board – I'm quite inexperienced in that respect, but I've known Yorrie for many years and know that she's a good yachtswoman; so that's one more point in favour of me agreeing to be your skipper.'

By the time he had finished, Henro's fingers were all clenched into a tight fist, with which he tapped slowly and rhythmically on the table. He started banging it harder and harder, as if to say: 'Right, enough of this chatter. Let's get down to work!'

'Let's allocate what needs to be done to get to sea. We haven't got much time left,' he proposed.

And he was right. Time really was running out. A friend of mine from the Bulgarian Press Agency's Balkan Department, who had undertaken to keep track of Tim Severin's expedition by following foreign press agency reports and reports in the Greek and Turkish papers, had just told me that the galley *Argo* had successfully passed through the Bosphorus, managing to row against the strong current there. Tim Severin was already in the Black Sea! And he was only three days behind schedule. Would we also manage to set sail in time to get to Georgia and meet up with *Argo*? We wouldn't have the Bosphorus to contend with, but we still had to deal with quite a few organisational counter-currents to get our expedition aboard the *Aurora* underway.

The days leading up to our departure became a giddy succession of relief at solving one problem alternating with despair as another seemingly insoluble hitch came up. It was only late at night that I would be able to snatch a few minutes to scribble down a few lines in my diary:

1 July. Today the Argonautica Expedition should have set sail, at least according to the official schedule which I had prepared to make the crew hurry up.

Instead, the yacht is still in dry dock, Yorrie and I spending all day sanding and varnishing the decks. Milen and Sasho also give us a hand, even though they're not on the crew, and are merely helping for the pleasure of doing something for the expedition. But there are no other members of the crew around: Sergei is still in Sofia, Misho is pottering about on some digs, and nobody knows where the Varna crew have got to. In the evening Henro turned up from a wedding, no less, and gave us a quick hand before nightfall. Tomorrow we'll see whether the expedition will be or not be. There is no crew as yet!

Old Roissa seems to have been right – the most difficult thing about an expedition *is* getting a crew together. If everybody had been here and done their part of the work, at least we'd have the yacht afloat instead of propped up in dry dock.

2 July. The expedition is on after all! I've sorted out the passports, and at long last the funds donated by *Echo* have arrived, after being sent off from Sofia two weeks ago – God only knows what bureaucratic tangles they got themselves tied up in before reaching us.

The only thing I can't see yet is the crew – they just don't seem able to get together, full stop. Misho is still on his digs, as if he expects to make a new discovery any moment now. The others from Varna are still at work, getting their leave sorted out. Only Petyo is now working on the yacht.

THE ARGONAUTICA EXPEDITION

In the evening I finally managed to get everyone together for a serious talk in the Golden Wheel. Things are beginning to move...

3 July. A big problem has cropped up in the transport company. Their director has refused to allow Henro and Stoyan to go on leave, out of the blue. It seems he was suddenly afraid that the expedition really would materialise. I couldn't believe my ears when I heard him explain that the yacht wasn't suitable for such lengthy cruises all the way across the Black Sea... because it would wear out. And that she was only suitable for short cruises in Varna Bay.

This evening we worked on the yacht till late. At least we're all together now, even though Henro seems a bit down, and can't think of a way of getting his boss to let them go. He just sits there, sighing and shaking his head: 'Well, what do you expect? We're just stuck out in the provinces here. They won't let you sail over to the other side of the puddle, and God forbid if you start thinking of a round-the-world voyage...'

4 July. We're still working on the yacht, but at least now the end's in sight. About their leave, no news yet. And time's moving fast.

The Plovdiv sailor Dr Garo Tomasyan gave me the number of a friend of his who lives in Poti. We managed to get through to him, and he told us that they were expecting Tim Severin there on 20 July. High time we set sail! Henro, Misho and I have been thinking about alternative routes.

5 July. At long last Henro and Stoyan have got permission for leave. In the afternoon we all worked on the yacht – she's now painted, varnished and rigged. *Aurora* is becoming more and more handsome every day. When will we finally be able to get her afloat?

6 July. We're already filling in the crew list for the voyage. Sergei vanished somewhere early this morning, so we filled out his form for him. We're six yachtsmen and one 'passenger', and he's a Soviet national. I wonder what the Turkish and Soviet customs officers will make of that?

7 July. Hooray! A crane came along and lifted *Aurora* into the water. We spent our time till late afternoon clearing out the things we wouldn't need. Then we sailed her over to the quay opposite the

THE CREW

Transport Company's marina, and started loading provisions in the evening.

8 July. It's Sunday – today we set sail. Friends have come from Varna, Sofia and Plovdiv to see us off.

In the morning we continued to load on stores, and at noon we used the engine to go up the canal to the seaport. It's almost a year since my last expedition to Malta. I looked at Sergei: 'We're off, at long last!' He replied: 'Don't count your chickens – wait until we've rounded Cape Galata!'

It took an hour or two for the frontier officials to arrive. Meanwhile our friends were saying goodbye, photographers snapped away and journalists tried to conduct last-minute interviews with us.

And then – a slap in the face! One of the border officials noticed that Yorrie's passport had only a Black Sea visa, instead of an All Seas and Oceans visa.

'Well, we're going to sail in the Black Sea, aren't we?'

'Yes, but you'll be passing along the Turkish coast of the Black Sea, and you need an All Seas and Oceans visa for there.'

'Do you mean to say that the Asia Minor shore of the Black Sea isn't the Black Sea?'

'Sorry, but rules are rules.'

'But the passports of all of us from Sofia were handed in together – somebody there can't have known about your rules and stamped in different visas for the same expedition.'

'Even if that is the case, the young lady, nice though she is, can't leave with you until we get instructions for an All Seas and Oceans visa for her from Sofia.'

Henro and I looked at each other. He made a desperate final attempt to get us out of this quandary. 'Okay, what if we decide to sail straight across to Georgia and not follow the coast of Asia Minor, will we all be able to sail together then?'

'Yes, but you told us earlier that you intend to follow the Turkish Black Sea coast. Now if you hadn't told us that . . .'

Henro sighed deeply and decided to postpone the expedition by one day to try to sort things out. Then he remembered his earlier suggestion that we sail down to Istanbul and meet up with Tim Severin there and sail for the rest of the voyage together. At the time we had turned down his suggestion, because there hadn't been the time to arrange it all. But if we had accepted it we wouldn't be having all the problems with the visas now, since Istanbul is outside the Black Sea for our passport officials. Henro summed it all up in a remarkable aphorism: 'To get to Georgia one has to pass through Constantinople.'

9 July. We're still in Varna, still at the seaport, although yesterday the press, radio and television had announced our departure – they had gone by the time the border officials arrived.

An endless day of ringing up Sofia time and time again to try to get the machinery started that would be able to telex an All Seas and Oceans visa for Yorrie.

The tension reached its peak in the evening – the crew were all hanging about on the yacht waiting, while Misho Lazarov shook his head slowly, saying, 'Well, it looks as if you'll be sailing without me.' The longer we delayed, the less time there would be for the coast of Asia Minor, which was the most interesting part for him as a historian. He had visited all the sites in Georgia already. Henro grumbled that the entire crew would fall apart if we didn't get going as soon as possible. Sofia for its part had made it clear that the telex wouldn't get here before tomorrow. Stoyan stood up for Yorrie, saying that it could have happened to any one of us. Sergei insisted on waiting, while Petyo was in two minds about it. My situation was particularly delicate – after all, Yorrie was my wife, but as head of the expedition I didn't want to be seen as showing any favouritism. So I decided that we would wait until 10 a.m. the next day, and if there was no result we'd set sail without her.

I stayed up on deck all night. I just couldn't get to sleep. The spiteful voice of the chief of some department in Sofia whom I'd been on the phone to kept echoing through my head: 'Don't worry, just use the extra time to improve your scientific programmes, count the stars, eat some plankton . . .' That was the extent of his knowledge about expeditions, and he was probably now very pleased with himself over his witty answer to these upstart mariners from Sofia.

If Jason had had to rely on him for his visa to Colchis three thousand years ago, the Argonauts would probably have had to call their expedition off, and might still be there to this day counting stars in Volos.

10 July. Early in the morning, after another round of telephone calls, I managed to reach the secretary of one of the most important departments concerned with our case. She turned out to be very understanding, and promised to get things moving at once. As I counted the minutes that remained until 10 o'clock, some friends from the lifeboat *Neptun* came aboard to pay us a visit. They brought us the day's issue of *Otechestven Vestnik*, with an article about our expedition. 'Are they going to announce your departure every day now?' they asked.

Ten o'clock was approaching. I nipped over to the yacht club, where Yorrie was hovering over the telephone – I wished that somebody would finally ring up and give her some good news. I could see how upset she was at the prospect of having to stay behind just because of some bureaucratic slip, after we'd been together all this time dealing with one problem after another and getting the expedition ready. At 10 sharp we looked at each other and she shrugged her shoulders. I turned round and walked towards the yacht to tell Henro to go and call the border officials so that we could start off without Yorrie.

I walked slowly up to the quay, and just before I reached *Aurora* someone gave a piercing whistle behind me. I turned round. Yorrie was standing on the terrace of the clubhouse, waving her arms excitedly with her fingers in the skin-divers' 'OK' sign. OK! The telex had just come through. As Yorrie rushed over to get her new visa stamped into her passport (I'd never thought that she could run so fast), Henro called the border guards. This time the formalities were over quite quickly and in about half an hour we were throwing the lines over to the quay. Yorrie just couldn't believe that we really were setting off with the whole crew aboard – she kept looking back, expecting to see a motorboat roaring after us to call us back over some other little formality. We let her take first watch at the wheel, so that she could assure herself that we really had put to sea, and, when Cape Galata was astern, Sergei produced a bottle of champagne which exploded triumphantly, the cork almost hitting Henro, who was helping Petyo and Stoyan to prepare the sails for raising. Sergei yelled in Russian, 'We're off!', and rushed over to help them raise the sails, mixing up in his excitement the mainstays and jib-sheets. Petyo tactfully moved him aside so that he could calm down a little.

In the afternoon the sun showed from behind the clouds. We were now on course for the shore of Asia Minor. There was a fair wind blowing, and we were making a speed of 4 to 5 knots. We all agreed not to mention the events of the last few days any more. We were at sea now, and that demanded a new rhythm of life and promised new experiences.

6

AURORA IN THE PONTUS

'At the time of Homer,' writes the Greek geographer and historian Strabo in his work *Geographia*, 'people considered the Pontian Sea to be a second ocean and believed that the people who sailed upon it came from beyond the limits of the known world, as did those who sailed beyond the Pillars of Hercules.[1] As the Pontian Sea was thought to be the greatest of all seas in our part of the known world, it was given the unusual name Pontus, in the same way as Homer himself was known as the "poet".'

It seems that in ancient days, as in our own time, people used their own experience of the world as the yardstick by which to measure it. Now we, too, were unfurling our sails to see what we could find out about the early history of the Black Sea, or the Pontus, as it was called then. A mere blue dot on the map in comparison with the world's great oceans, it would have to be regarded by us as 'the greatest of all seas' if we wanted to play our role as travellers in the ancient Pontus.

This would be Misho Lazarov's first experience of sailing in the open sea. He would also be the first Bulgarian archaeologist to visit the Black Sea coast of Asia Minor. And the *Aurora* would

[1] Gibraltar.

be one of the first Bulgarian yachts to sail in this region. Previously Captain Demerdjiev had sailed only as far as Sinop along the ancient navigation route, whence he had turned due north to sail across the narrowest part of the Black Sea.

Thoughts like this kept running through my head during my first night-watch as the *Aurora* cut through the darkness not caring that her role as an ancient sailing ship probably would have prevented her from sailing against the wind. Henro was pleased by the speed she was making, while Misho kept switching on his torch to see how the sails were doing; he evidently wanted to see the degree to which a modern yacht could sail into the wind.

Actually only Henro, Yorrie and I were really supposed to be on watch; Petyo and Sergei would take over from us, followed by Stoyan and Misho, and then it would be the first ones' turn again. Henro had decided the rota of four-hour watches. But everyone's excitement at the fact that the expedition was finally underway meant that nobody wanted to sleep on the first night. The captain had also been responsible for designating the bunks. The two bunks in the bow were for Yorrie and myself, so that we'd be rocked hardest by the waves and see what it really was like to be ancient seafarers. In the middle section were the neatest and untidiest members of our expedition, Stoyan and Sergei; these two extremes had been put together so that their part of the ship would more or less conform to the standards of tidiness that an expedition requires. And on the single bunk in the living quarters would rest the scientific brains of the expedition in the person of Misho; he needed room for his imagination and as the eldest, and supposedly also the most restrained of all of us, had to keep the 'liquid gold' under his bunk in case we finished it all off before reaching the land of the Golden Fleece, where it might come in handy as a means of exchange. And right at the stern the so-called graveyard bunks on either side of the rudder would be for Petyo and Henro – so they could be nearest to the way out to the deck, to the navigator's table, and to the food stores. It is important that the captain and the navigator should never go hungry, since that might make them impatient and explosive and generally upset the balance of life aboard.

Yorrie was pleased to be so far from the galley. Her greatest fear about taking part in the expedition didn't concern her sailing skills or the fact that she was the only woman aboard, which she had been on the Malta expedition, as much as the fear of being made to cook. Our one year's matrimony had not been enough to verse her in this art, in which I myself hadn't even scratched the surface. So she was delighted when on the first day of the expedition she heard the captain say, as he allocated the duties:

'Cooking to be done by whoever enjoys doing it.'

'Now that's what I call psychological compatibility!' Yorrie exclaimed, and took Petyo's place at the wheel when he decided to cook our first supper.

After the evening meal we all went over to the cockpit around the wheel, as that was the most convenient place to get together on deck; elsewhere, the superstructure left only two narrow lanes leading to the bow, which had to be kept clear for manning the sails.

A fresh breeze was still blowing, and Misho beside me was huddled in his anorak, only his nose showing from the hood. I peered in to make sure that he hadn't dozed off.

'Theo, do you know what our biggest problem is? Apart from the stone anchors that we keep discovering on our coast and the Greek myths, there's nothing else to tell us about the time of the Argonauts, as you call it, in the Black Sea.'

I liked listening to Misho debating with imagined opponents, even though I already knew many of his conclusions from his book *The Sunken Flotilla* and other publications of his.

'Usually, when the question of navigation here in antiquity is discussed, what is stressed are the unfavourable atmospheric conditions, such as thick fogs, frequent overclouding, continual north winds and sudden storms. And to all this we should add the strong currents in the Bosphorus. I have been told that they present a serious challenge even to modern yachtsmen.'

'Yes, I remember. Last year, when we came back from Malta, we had to get a Bulgarian ship to tow us up the Bosphorus because the engine wasn't powerful enough.'

'Exactly. But many scholars today seem to overestimate the navigational difficulties this presents, and so jump to the conclusion that it was impossible for sailors from other places to enter the Black Sea before navigation had developed and high-speed rowing craft such as the trireme had been invented.'

'You mean the ships with triple rows of oars.'

'That's right. Which takes us back no earlier than the beginning of mass Greek colonisation, because according to Thucydides the trireme was introduced to navigation around the year 700 BC.'

'Actually, the British have recently said that they intend to re-create an Athenian trireme. Scholars from Cambridge have designed it, and it'll be built in Piraeus with the help of the Greek navy. Then they'll make some experimental voyages.'

'That's interesting. You should find out some more details. But to get back to the stone anchors we were just discussing...'

And Misho got back on to his favourite subject. About twenty years ago in the western part of the bay of Cape Kaliakra, members of a skin-diving expedition came up with a square stone slab containing three holes. A year later, divers on an expedition organised by the Bourgas museum found two trapezium-shaped slabs with two symmetrical holes on each in the Bay of Sozopol. This was the beginning of a large number of similar finds, and to date Bulgarian submarine archaeologists have discovered more than two hundred stone anchors, the largest collection so far.

'But they're nothing new,' Misho went on. 'Anchors like that are known throughout the Mediterranean. Some time ago I saw similar anchors from the Atlantic coast of Spain which bear a surprising resemblance to those found in the Black Sea.'

'An archaeologist I met last year in Malta told me that even today some fishermen in the Mediterranean use stones as anchors.'

'That's right. I remember how, when the first ones were discovered, many people denied that they were ancient at all, saying they were simply stones like the ones used by present-day fishermen. It's a very old tradition. If we follow it back in literature, we can go back to Homer. If you look in the *Odyssey*, for instance, it says that when the boat carrying Penelope's admirers landed in Ithaca the sailors lowered a stone anchor. And the *Iliad* mentions a stone anchor on the ship with which Ulysses returned Chryseis to her father Chrysis, the priest of Apollo, after she had been captured by Agamemnon.'

'So if at the time of the Trojan War stone anchors were commonplace, we can easily relate the ones found off the Bulgarian coast to the time of the Argonauts. When I was talking with Zara Gocheva a few months ago she mentioned that the Argonauts' expedition couldn't have taken place more than a generation before the Trojan War.'

Misho shrugged:

'Well, that has been accepted, mainly because of Laertes, Ulysses' father. Laertes is mentioned among the Argonauts, and afterwards his son is one of the main heroes of the Trojan War. But the ancients themselves dated the Argonauts to the Mycenaean age, calling them Mynes or Pelasges, which were tribes of the Creto-Mycenaean age, that is, the second millennium BC. The age of the anchors themselves is still being debated, but the predominant view is that they were used mainly during the second millennium BC. And so it's no coincidence that the archaeological data coincide with the references in mythology and those given by ancient authors. In fact, while the tale of the Argonauts involves just a single voyage along the Black Sea coast, our archaeological discoveries presuppose regular shipping there. The stone anchors which we've discovered so far on the western coast come from several regions and are so grouped that they definitively show the existence of ancient ports or at least regular places of anchorage. The fact that large numbers are found in one place can only be the result of regular shipping along definite routes and ports.'

Sergei, who had been listening attentively to our conversation from the other side of the cockpit, intervened:

'As far as I remember about forty anchors were found in the bays around Sozopol, and twenty off Nessebur.'

'You might have taken part in submarine expeditions,' Misho laughed, 'but your facts are a bit out of date. More than fifty anchors have been found off Sozopol and twenty-five off Nessebur, which had harbours on both sides of the peninsula in ancient times, unlike now. From Kaliakra, where you found your ingot, we've recovered about twenty anchors. And it's the same with other places, such as Kavarna Bay and Cape Shabla, for instance. Also don't forget that the anchors we find are only a small proportion of the anchors that were actually lowered – they're only the ones that for various reasons did not come up again.'

'And most of these places were around Greek colonies,' Sergei intervened.

'Not just Greek,' Misho interrupted, 'but earlier. The places that we've studied so far were all near ancient ports: the Bay of Sozopol was called Apollonia Pontica, but the Nessebur Peninsula used to be the Thracian town of Melsebria, which only became a Greek colony afterwards. Kavarna used to be Bizone in Thracian times, while Kaliakra was the Thracian settlement of Tyrisis inhabited by the Tyrisi tribe, and Shabla is presumed to have been the ancient port of Karon Limen. Both archaeologists and linguists agree that these ports are very old, which puts paid to the theory that in Thracian times sea-voyages in the Black Sea were rare. As during the second millennium BC the coast was known to the people of the eastern Mediterranean, the myth of the Argonauts was probably not mere fantasy, but the result of their knowledge of navigation in the Black Sea.'

The next morning, when my watch came round again, I caught Misho dozing in the cockpit. I didn't know whether he had gone to his bunk at all after our conversation of the previous night. The moment I appeared to take the wheel, Stoyan rushed off, taking care not to wake the scientific director, to change the jib for a lighter one. The wind had fallen a lot and was changing direction from south-east to south.

Henro slipped out of his 'grave', climbed up the steps and stuck his dishevelled head out above the deck to see which way the wind was blowing. Then he turned towards the bow, where Stoyan was grappling with the jib single-handed.

'Blooper, what're we going to do with this piddly speed? It had to be your watch, didn't it? The scientific director dropped off and we missed the forecast.'

Misho opened his eyes and stood up to see who the captain was talking to. It was Stoyan, because nobody else on board could have the nickname of a sail. He grinned good-naturedly, and moved the foresheet of the lighter jib. Misho jumped up to help him, although Blooper had just about finished. But this reassured the captain that the 'scientific director', despite his academic titles and superiority in years over the rest, wouldn't start taking on airs and sitting like a piece of luggage throughout the expedition.

Petyo also jumped out into the cockpit, wearing just the shorts he had slept in, looked behind him into the cabin, and hastily straightened the not-all-that-abundant hair on his head, saying, 'Blooper, go and spruce yourself up and put your fresh shorts on, the only lady aboard is coming up!'

'Oh, stop fussing about me and just relax, will you? I thought we'd agreed that there wouldn't be men and women aboard, just crew members,' she said, taking over from me at the wheel.

'You're right there,' Henro muttered into his moustache. 'Things have got mixed up enough as it is – women at the helm, men cooking and washing up . . . Hey, Misho, is that what things were like at the time of the Argonauts?'

But Misho was busy in the galley making up a salad of olives and onion to an ancient recipe which had miraculously remained unchanged through the ages – in ingredients, method and manner of consumption, i.e. with grape brandy. When Sergei heard the word 'cooking' he immediately came up with the suggestion that we proceed with dishes of different nations, and after this ancient Greek salad offered to risk knocking up a Tatar *azu* for supper. At first it wasn't too clear where exactly the risk element lay until, after rummaging around in all corners of the yacht for a whole hour in places where the ingredients couldn't – or rather shouldn't – be kept, he called out from the bunk-locker with the spare sails:

'Do you know what I still need?'

Yorrie anticipated him, remembering the previous voyage.

'Yes, we know. Bay-leaves. And peas. Lashings of peas.'

'Precisely! And where can I find them on this yacht? Here

The golden ingot in the shape of a sheepskin, discovered in the Black Sea, led to a new hypothesis concerning the origins of the Golden Fleece.

Stone anchors, found in the Black Sea, are evidence of active navigation at the time of the Argonauts.

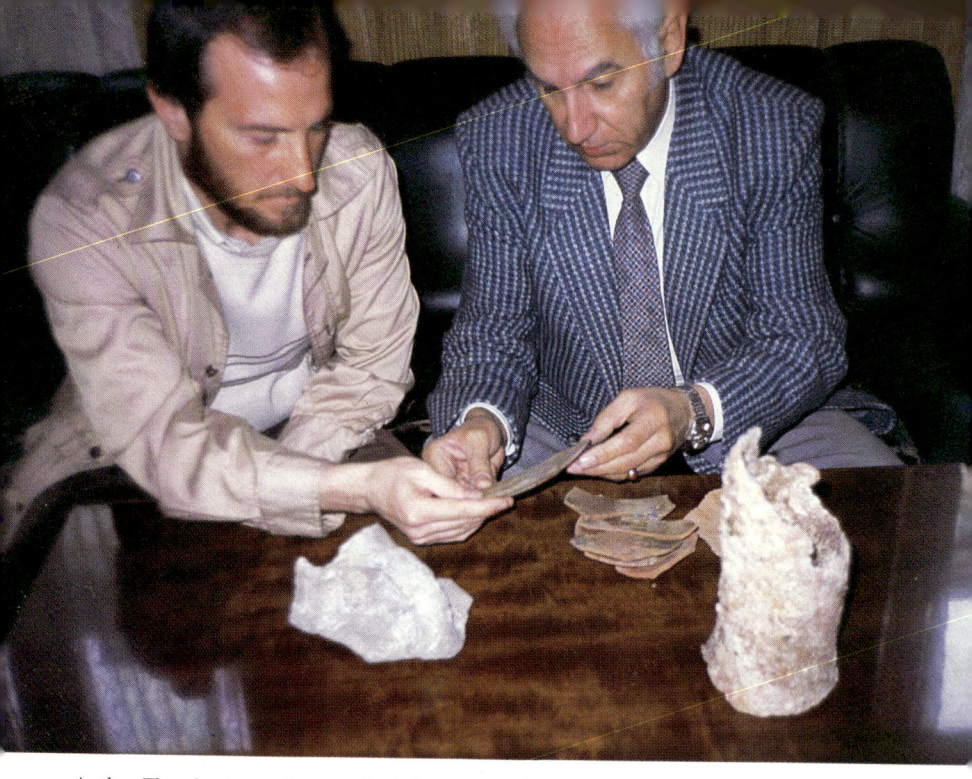

Author Theodor Troev (*left*) worked closely with Professor Velizar Velkov, head of the Archaeological Institute in Sofia, in planning the Argonautica Expedition

The legend of Jason, Medea and the Argonauts is a traditional theme for Georgian artists, as in this mural painting in the Phasis Academy at Poti

The flower of Orpheus in the Rhodope mountains, where, it is said, the master musician and key member of Jason's team had his home

Generations of talented folk musicians have kept alive the myth of Orpheus in the Rhodope mountains

The Argonautica Expedition setting out from the Black Sea port of Varna

Above: In Colchis, present-day Georgia, the Bulgarian team met with *Argo*, a reconstruction of a Bronze Age galley, aboard which the renowned explorer Tim Severin was tracing the route of Jason

Left: A symbolic image of the art of Orpheus, the Thracian Argonaut, was presented to the crew of the modern *Argo* by the Bulgarian expedition

Below: *Argo*, as if emerging from the millennia, accompanied by the Russian training ship *Tovarishch*

The author telling Tim Severin about the golden ingot and other archaeological discoveries relating to ancient navigation in the Black Sea

Fair winds for *Argo* on arrival on the coast of Georgia

Ruins of a temple near Kutaisi, the Georgian town claiming to h[ave been home to] Aeetes, who owned the Golden Fleece

Reliefs in old Georgian temples are a reminder of ancient glories

Homeward bound aboard the *Aurora*, following the return route of *Argo*. Archaeologist Mikhail Lazarov relaxes while Maria Troev takes the wheel. In the background is the author

everything is so tidied. On the other yacht, there were tins of food everywhere – just where I needed them.'

The *azu* really did prove a big surprise, not just for the crew members who tried it for the first time, but even for those of us who knew it in all its varieties from our dozen or so previous voyages with Sergei: with and without meat, with and without potatoes, with and without sauce, boiled, fried or baked, but always with lashings of peas and bay-leaves. Only the reaction of the other chef aboard, Petyo, was hard to understand. I watched with concern as he started crawling on all fours from one cabin to another, burrowing like a mole into the farthest corners of the yacht – corners whose existence I hadn't even suspected. Only later, through Sergei's wails or delighted exclamations of discovery, did I realise that Petyo had simply been trying to bridle Sergei's culinary imagination by stowing the tinned peas and bay-leaves as far away as possible.

Petyo had another cause for concern right at the outset. As navigator, he had agreed to keep the ship's log, by writing down daily her course, wind speed and direction, condition of sea, watches, etc. But, painstaking to the extreme, he also decided to add to all these details every change of sails – just in case the scientific director and the captain needed them later for analytical purposes.

But Petyo hadn't reckoned with Blooper. It was Stoyan's first trip aboard *Aurora*, and right from the start he had decided to squeeze as much speed as possible from the craft. And the slightest alteration in the wind was enough to make him – whether on watch or not – change a sail or two, be it to replace the ordinary jib for a Genoa jib, or to lower the mizzen-sail, or to slacken the mainsail. This didn't always have a palpable effect on the yacht's pace, but for Blooper the main thing was for there to be movement on deck, and to keep on trying to obtain a better speed.

And now, as we were recovering, lying sprawled on deck, from Sergei's first *cordon bleu* onslaught, Petyo kept having to rush down to the navigator's table where the ship's log was to record Blooper's latest attempt – for in the past hour or so the wind had blown up and dropped several times, each time provoking an immediate reaction from Stoyan. In the end, the navigator couldn't take any more of these endless gymnastic displays.

'Come on Misho, can't you tell this mad inventor what they did in the old days when they had only a single square sail?'

'Yes, what did they do?' Stoyan asked, looking up.

'They waited, that's what they did! They waited for a decent wind to blow up, so that they could sail like normal human beings!'

'Don't worry yourself about old Blooper,' Henro intervened with a magnanimous smile on his face. 'He's still young and green, he still runs after girls, he's not like us. That's why he's in a hurry to get the cruise over with, because they're probably already waiting for him on shore.'

But Petyo wouldn't give in that easily.

'Okay, but what will this log look like in a a few days' time – "raise jib, lower jib, raise jib, lower jib . . ." The same thing every half an hour, and not the slightest difference in wind speed. We'll become a laughing-stock if anyone decides to read it.'

'Well, don't bother putting it in, then,' Sergei advised him. 'Just write "Blooper", and we'll all understand what it means.'

'And when I write "Sergei", it'll mean "reduction of ballast in the form of tinned peas".'

Misho Lazarov got up to stretch his legs a bit. In the last weeks before we set sail, he had been rushing around from one excavation site to another all the time, and now he found it a bit cramped in the limited space of the yacht, and had not as yet found something to while away the time as Stoyan had. Sailing on the open sea wasn't all that interesting, and he resignedly waited for the next day, when we'd reach the coast of Asia Minor. At one stage he asked Henro:

'Captain, the wind seems to have dropped, so why don't we lower the sails for a bit and go for a swim in the clean water out here? After all, we're still a long way from the coast, aren't we?'

Henro was just wondering whether to agree or not when Blooper shielded his eyes with his hand and looked out to port.

'We're not that far away at all. There's the shore, over there!'

'Come off it! You're pulling my leg!'

'We're not a speedboat to get there so quickly!'

'Look at him, he's having us on!'

Without saying another word, Stoyan picked up the binoculars and without even looking through them passed them over to Misho. Misho took them cautiously, wondering whether he was about to fall for it or not, and suddenly exclaimed:

'Hey, the lad's right! Captain, what is going on here?'

We all jumped to our feet. To port we really could make out, albeit unclearly, the outline of land on the horizon. Yes, there was no doubt about it. Petyo got out his charts of the Turkish coast, but it was too far away for us to take any exact bearings.

Misho Lazarov, and for that matter the rest of us, continued to wonder how we had managed to reach the shores of Asia Minor so quickly, when we saw a light object bobbing up and down on the waves somewhere to the side, going in the same direction as we were going. It was a beach-ball. From which shore of the Black Sea had it come? We noticed something like advertising slogans on it. Misho insisted that we approach it and pick it up. We started up the engines, because there was almost no wind, but the ball was continuing to move. When we drew close to it, Sergei decided to dive in and throw it up to us, so that he could swim around the yacht a few times. Misho immediately examined it with interest.

'It's from Constanta,' he announced. 'Now I'm even more confused. Where on earth could we be?'

It was only after dark, when we could make out the lights of various lighthouses, that we realised that we were off the coast of Asia Minor somewhere between the towns of Eregli and Zonguldak. Petyo, Misho and Henro started calculating aloud how we had travelled. It appeared that our average speed had been 6 knots, which was normal for a modern yacht like *Aurora*, even though it seemed a trifle fast to us.

'Misho, what would things have been like in an ancient tub under these conditions?' asked Henro.

'Well, the average speed of ancient traders was about four knots.'

'How did they work it out?'

'By taking the total time taken for long hauls – from Rhodes to the Danube, for instance. But what I wonder is, how would it have been on different legs of the route with favourable winds and currents? In our case, the wind has been south and south-east, which doesn't really pose a problem to a modern yacht, but it would have been very difficult for an ancient sailing vessel. So that leaves the current. The current that flows southwards along the western shore of the Black Sea, and then flows eastwards. But the question is – could the current also have helped us in our modern yacht to get from Varna to Eregli so quickly? Perhaps the current is precisely what determined the ancient route from Odessos to Heraclea Pontica. And look at the ball we've just found: it also demonstrates the importance of the current, which I think is also responsible for bringing us out here.'

'What ancient route?' asked Petyo.

'I'm just wondering whether we haven't stumbled across the

route used by the ancients when they sailed from Odessos, or Varna, to Heraclea Pontica, which is today Eregli in Turkey,' explained Misho Lazarov. 'Heraclea used to trade with ports along the western shore. In Varna there is a lot of evidence, mainly in the form of amphorae, which indicates regular trading links between the two cities. Of course, it would be too hasty to jump to conclusions from just this one attempt, but it seems to me that the direct route between Odessos and Heraclea Pontica deserves more attention and should be tried out.'

When Misho mentioned Heraclea Pontica, I remembered the notes I had made when reading *Argonautica*. Apollonius of Rhodes mentions this region when he describes the cave of the god of the underworld Hades, the mouth of the river Acheron and the Acherusian Cape, beyond which the Argonauts anchored. They were received well by the tribe of the Mariandyne, enemies of the Bebryces tribe, because one of the Argonauts, Pollux, had in a previous episode during the voyage killed the king of the Bebryces, Amycus, in a boxing match. The Bebryces erected a monument to the twins Castor and Pollux, which would serve as a landmark for all those who sailed along the Argonauts' route. This is not surprising, as in ancient mythology, which Apollonius knew well, the brothers Dioscuri (sons of Zeus) were known as saviours of shipwrecked seafarers, and thus were worshipped by sailors. The Dioscurans revealed their presence by making small flames at the tops of the masts of ships, which are in fact caused by atmospheric electricity during storms.

This episode in the Argonauts' voyage is much more down to earth and realistic than the labours which Hercules performed in the same region. This was the place where Hercules had descended into the underworld to bring back its terrible guard, the three-headed dog Cerberus, from whose saliva the poisonous flower Aconitum penetrated into the soil. The plant

THE ARGONAUTICA EXPEDITION

really does grow near Eregli and is used by folk-healers. And the present name of Eregli is in fact a modern corruption of the original name, Heracles.

I looked with interest at the charts of the region. Even if we had wanted to stop off where the Argonauts had once anchored according to Apollonius, we wouldn't have been able to, for the area is now a military zone. I hoped that Tim Severin would be able to stop there, since his crew included Turkish rowers, and identify some of the landmarks described by Apollonius.

Actually, I didn't know why I was thinking in the future tense. Tim Severin had entered the Black Sea with *Argo* on 15 June. However slowly he progressed, if everything ran smoothly, he would have passed the same place ten days later. And where could he be now? I got out the chart of the eastern Black Sea coast of Turkey and tried to estimate how far *Argo* might have got. I wasn't sure whether the galley had stopped every night, or pressed on if there was a fair wind. One way or another, Tim Severin should now be somewhere between Ordu and Trabzon. Which meant that it was likely that in about four days' time we would catch up with *Argo* on her way to Georgia.

After midnight the wind dropped completely, and we decided to go on under engine-power; there was no point in hanging around all night in one place and wasting time, particularly if there was a likelihood of meeting up with *Argo* soon. The monotonous hum of the engine soon made me feel drowsy. I started imagining introducing myself to Tim Severin, and joining the modern Argonauts on their way to Colchis . . .

Suddenly a loud rattle came from the engine, quickly waking me up again. Henro stood beside me in the cockpit.

'What's happening?' asked Yorrie, who was at the wheel at that moment.

'That's a question I wish I could answer,' muttered Henro. 'Can you?'

The engine had suddenly stopped, and now all that could be heard was a strange whistling. Henro switched off the ignition, but the whistling continued. It didn't take Stoyan, as a professional driver and mechanic, long to conclude: 'The connection between the reverse clutch and the crankshaft has gone.'

'What's that whistling, then?'

'That's the screw, continuing to turn in the current.'

'And slipping out towards the rudder,' added Petyo.

'That's bad,' said Henro thoughtfully. 'If we don't manage to stop the screw from turning somehow, it could smash the rudder.'

'And then neither Castor, nor Pollux, nor anyone else will be able to help us.'

'That's funny, isn't it? The engine breaking down on the yacht provided by the Motor Company. It's a good thing we've got drivers aboard to repair it.'

'It's not as simple as you think,' said Stoyan. 'We can't just botch up a clutch here.'

'Obviously Blooper wants us to sail just on wind-power,' said Misho.

'It's no joke, it looks as if we'll have to carry on under sail,' Henro said gruffly. 'If there's any wind . . .'

About two hours later, when the lads had just managed to tie ropes around the screw-shaft to stop it from turning in the water and prevent it from piercing the rudder, a breeze blew up. It was just right for us, as the captain had decided to change course in the circumstances and to head due north-east in order to avoid ending up on unknown shores. So we ballooned the sails, letting them out on both sides. From now on we really would be carrying on like the ancients, relying solely on wind-power. Even *Argo* had the advantage of its twenty oars to help it along in a lull.

I sensed that Henro was worried. The seal of the propellor-shaft was beginning to let in water, which meant that it had to be pumped out regularly. The captain went down to the navigator's table several times, looked carefully at the charts of the Turkish coast, had consultations with Petyo, and finally said:

'Theo, what do you say we head straight for Poti?'

Before I managed to answer, Misho Lazarov did:

'How about putting in at the nearest Turkish harbour to fix the engine and then carrying on?'

'That's just what I want to avoid,' said Henro, stroking his beard. 'In my view it's risky putting in at an unknown harbour with a broken-down engine without being sure that we'll find a workshop able to get a new clutch together quickly. And if we are overtaken by stormy weather and the wind's against us, we risk being caught in a trap and being unable to carry on at all. That could upset the whole schedule of the expedition, and we might even miss meeting up with Tim Severin in Georgia.'

'If I don't see Sinop, Samsun and Trabzon on the Asia Minor coast, I might as well not have come at all,' Misho grumbled.

We quickly had to come to a decision that would satisfy both sides before the atmosphere aboard became poisoned. The captain was right as far as getting to Georgia to meet up with *Argo* on time was concerned. But Misho was also right: if we skipped the coast of Asia Minor, half of the expedition would be ruined. There was only one way out:

'Well, why don't we carry on along the Turkish coast now,' I suggested, 'so Misho can get a general impression of it, and then, when we reach Inceburun, which is just before Sinop, take a short cut across to Poti so that we can get to Georgia at about the same time as *Argo*. And when we've completed our programme in Georgia, instead of heading straight for Varna, we could go back along the coast of Asia Minor stopping off at Trabzon, Samsun and Sinop, because we'll get the engine done in Poti. In that way, we'll also be following the Argonauts' return route, according to Apollonius. And after that we'll be sailing up towards Varna by the route which the Argonauts took along the western shores of the Black Sea when they were travelling to Istros, or the Danube.'

This idea was accepted. Petyo went back to the navigating table to map out the new route, while those who weren't on watch went back to bed; in all the confusion and excitement of the night we hadn't noticed that it was beginning to get light. It started to drizzle, and the deck became slippery. Henro let out a line which trailed behind the yacht, just in case the worst happened and someone did go overboard; it would give them a chance of holding on. In this wind, and without an engine, it would be more difficult to manoeuvre and go about quickly if anything did happen.

By daylight we were already close to the coast of Asia Minor. Misho Lazarov kept his binoculars glued to his eyes.

'Just look at that, Theo . . . I've heard of this coastline, I've read about it, I've seen it in photos, but actually seeing it really is . . .'

He tailed off, unable to find a suitable adjective. The coastline really was majestic, rugged, awesome with its towering mountains which swooped straight down into the sea. In places, rivers which flowed into the sea had cut deep valleys. Usually there were signs of life in the valleys: narrow paths and cart-tracks winding along the hillsides, leading to groups of small wooden houses, barns and sheds standing in the moist greenery of the small riverside pastures. Here and there among the rocks of the little bays were the boats of local fishermen. In this rugged coastal landscape fishing and, indeed, just sailing looked like a pretty hazardous occupation.

Somewhere in these Anatolian mountains was the land of the Paphlagones, the grim warriors mentioned by Homer as allies of the Trojans. The Greeks called this land Paphlagonia. The history of these tribes goes back to the second millennium BC, and at the time of the Argonauts their fighting prowess was already widely known, as was their unwelcoming attitude towards strangers who came by sea. They controlled the entire coastline, which in any case was almost inaccessible with its rocky cliffs and dark towering mountains, their peaks shrouded in mist.

'Do you know that the Paphlagonians lived at the time of the famous Anatolian Hittite civilisation?' said Misho, continuing to admire the view to port. 'The Hittites are usually associated with the Mediterranean coast of Asia Minor, while practically nobody has touched upon their feats on the Black Sea coast. The capital of Chatusa, near the present-day village of Bogazkoy, was closer to the Black Sea than to the Mediterranean. In my view, the contacts of the Hittites with the Black Sea deserve closer scrutiny.'

'Does this have anything to do with the Argonauts?'

Misho put down his binoculars for a while and turned to me, grinning.

'I knew that you'd ask me that question. That's why I started talking about the Hittites. There is a Hittite myth about a sacred fleece which hung on a tree. And what do you think the tree was called?'

I shrugged my shoulders.

'Aeae!' Misho exclaimed, looking at me expectantly.

'The same name as the land of the Golden Fleece?'

'Precisely. In the Hittite myth, the fleece was actually a symbol given by the god to the king which served to illustrate the god's protection over the land. The cult of the Golden Fleece, which is characteristic rather of the northern parts of Anatolia, pre-dates even the Hittites, according to some historians. One way or another, this myth gives us a better idea of the Argonauts' quest for the Golden Fleece, for they found it in the land of Aeae, which was ruled by Aeetes, father of Medea and keeper of the Golden Fleece.'

Misho pulled his coat over his shoulders, for clouds again hid the sun, which had come out for a little while. Then he settled down comfortably in the cockpit, and went on:

'What I find interesting is the fact that the earliest authors who mention the Argonauts look for the land of Aeae somewhere in the Mediterranean. It wasn't until the fifth century BC that Herodotus redirected the Argonauts, as it were, towards Colchis. Perhaps he, as a very informed historian, came across the myth of the Golden Fleece in this part of the world. It's a myth that can be found in different versions among most Indo-European peoples, and it has strong traditions. Until recently it was also preserved in Svanetia, a region of Georgia, where people ritually slaughtered a bull or sheep, hanging the skin out on a sacred oak.'

'So the legend of the Golden Fleece is based on real facts . . .'

'Well, in this case it reflects some early links between Greeks and the Hittites, or proto-Hittites, or northern Anatolians. Because in all versions after Herodotus the voyage takes place along the shores of the Black Sea.'

'That's right. I remember talking with Ivan Marazov before we set out, and he said that some Bulgarian researchers were inclined to see Thracian elements in the emergence of the story of the Argonauts – not just in the person of Orpheus, but even before that . . .'

'Indeed, some people have drawn analogies: the golden-fleeced ram on which Phrixus and Helle flew to Colchis, for example, was born from the marriage between Poseidon and the Thracian princess Bysaltide – if you remember, there was a Thracian tribe known as the Bysaltae. In the same way, etymologically the name of Phrixus can be seen as coming from the Thracian Phrygian tribe. But that complicates things too much. I think that it simply shows us yet again that the Argonauts' voyage is of interest to us precisely because it implies the possibility of very early links between different parts of the ancient world.'

Misho again turned to the coast to observe a small inlet, which was almost cut into the looming rocks – it was the only place of refuge in bad weather which we had seen for some hours now. Anyway, it was big enough only for small boats, and could hardly accommodate a fishing smack. What kind of vessel could have sailed along these shores in the times which Strabo writes about, when the Black Sea was known as Axinus Pontus, or the 'unfriendly sea'?

Misho's thoughts on Phrixus and Helle brought to my mind a colleague from Zvenigorod in the Soviet Union to whom I had written in connection with the preparations for the Argonautica Expedition. Vasilii Galenko was a correspondent for the Soviet travel magazine *Vokrug Sveta*, a navigator by profession who was particularly interested in ancient navigation. Together with another Soviet rowing expedition enthusiast, Evgenii Smurgis, he had travelled on many different rivers, lakes and seas in small rowing-boats which he reckoned resembled those used by the first explorers of ancient times.

In one of his letters he had written that the design of rowing-boats was determined by the relationship between the weight of boat and the number of rowers, so that they were able to carry the boat out of the water in case of storms. Looking at the forbidding rocky coastline now, I was hard put to imagine what kind of boats the ancients must have had to be able to pull them ashore safely in these conditions! My colleague had mentioned something interesting he had read by the scholar Boris Peters, who claimed that, if we base our theories on the myth, we can assume that Phrixus and Helle's voyage to

Colchis – which they had obviously undertaken by sea, and not by air – had been in a hide coracle made of sheepskins. Strabo mentions that such craft were used once in Meotida (the Sea of Azov). And there are records of similar boats elsewhere in the ancient world. It would be interesting to see what Tim Severin thought of this – after all, his first expedition had been to sail a boat made of hides across the Atlantic. There could hardly be a greater expert on hide boats in the world today.

Galenko had also mentioned the likelihood that the first exploratory trips in the Pontus were carried out in special small boats which the Greeks called *Kamara* – this assumption again was based on Strabo. What was special about them was that both the bow and the stern were pointed and curved upwards, which meant that they could draw up on to the beach with either end. In addition, during storms, planks could be attached to the side of the boat to prevent it from being swamped by the waves. My colleague said that he and Smurgis had experimented with boats like this. He maintained that the ancients at first called the Black Sea 'unfriendly' because viewed from such small craft the sea really did look much more dangerous than from the deck of the big ships used during the time of Greek colonisation. It was then, according to Strabo, that the Greeks started calling the sea Pontus Euxinios, meaning 'hospitable sea'. So it is possible that the labels 'hospitable' and 'inhospitable' used by the ancients were due not so much to their actual knowledge of its shores, as most historians believe, but rather to the development of larger ships for military and trading operations.

I pestered Misho Lazarov with questions of this kind all day long, questions to which there was no clear-cut answer. Even Sergei became so engrossed listening to us, at the same time contemplating the majestic scenery that glided past the yacht, that he forgot to spring his latest culinary surprise on us. On the other hand, Henro and Petyo used the lulls in the wind to put a line over the side and to treat us to fresh fish *à la Anatolien*. For the first time during our trip Blooper had the pleasure of raising and lowering the spinnaker – the large, balloon-like sail in the bow – several times, as the wind was still behind us.

By evening we were off Inceburun, the northernmost cape of the Asia Minor shore, which is also the narrowest part of the Black Sea. From here northwards to the Crimea it is 150 nautical miles – less than we had to cover to get to Poti. There was not a light to be seen along the rocky coastline around the cape apart from that of the lighthouse itself. Soon Sinop lighthouse was to starboard, and there instead of continuing to follow the coastline, which went south-east, we would head across the open sea direct to Poti. The wind blew up again, and soon we were making a decent speed – about 6 knots.

Just after midnight we found out that it was Friday the thirteenth. The billowing spinnaker was pulling the yacht confidently ahead, the bow slicing through the waves, when without any warning there was a splash, and the yacht suddenly lost speed. In the darkness we couldn't immediately make out what had happened.

'The spinnaker halyard!' Blooper was the first to react, bounding over to the bow.

We all rushed over to his aid. The spinnaker, which had become unfastened, was writhing in all directions and just beginning to pull at the spinnaker-boom, which was crashing ominously against the side-stays, ready to flick one of us overboard any moment. Henro yelled at us to watch out, and with Petyo's help he managed to unfasten the spinnaker-boom, while Stoyan grappled with the braces, trying to haul the sail aboard.

The swell, which had been less noticeable while we were sailing quickly, now raised the nose of the yacht and smashed it into the water. The spinnaker got caught under the bow and was in danger of being ripped in two. Petyo saved it with his self-control: he made Sergei lie down on that part of the sail which was aboard to prevent the wind from lifting it up again, while Henro and Stoyan helped him haul the rest of it aboard.

'I told you not to leave the spinnaker up at night,' Petyo grumbled later on. 'But Blooper just can't leave things alone...'

But that was only the lesser evil. The fact that the spinnaker halyard had snapped was a warning to reduce the sail area, for soon the wind blew even stronger, chasing *Aurora* between higher and higher waves. All night a north-westerly wind blew stronger and stronger. On our new course straight towards Poti we had already left the coast far to starboard, and could no longer see any lights. Before turning in, Henro made us reef the mainsail, and told the next watch:

'Keep your eyes peeled. We could smash into the Georgian coast at the rate we're going!'

Of course, we weren't that close. According to our calculations, based on our course and log, by 10 o'clock the following morning we would be 255 nautical miles from Poti.

The wind continued to blow steadily for another twenty-four hours, but the following night the sails hung limply. So we lowered them, and for hours just drifted along. The waves threw the yacht up and down, rocking her first from nose to stern, and then from side to side. This violent rocking had an adverse effect on our appetites, and the next day our stomachs were unable to take Sergei's latest – pickle-water with potatoes, olives, onions, salami, and, of course, bay-leaves and lashings of peas. Sergei put our apathy down to a certain psycho-physiological disturbance caused by Petyo and his open malevolence towards peas. So he took upon himself the noble task of curing our apathy. This he did by demonstratively eating spoonfuls of his pickle-water stew throughout the day with the expression of a mortal upon whom the gods themselves had bestowed the honour of partaking of their nectar. His self-sacrifice had its effect – suddenly we all felt like eating, just as he had reached the bottom of the pan, by which time he was sitting, or rather squatting, behind the stern in godlike awe, contemplating the sea below him with Olympian indifference.

Even Misho Lazarov's spirits dropped with the wind. The continuous jokes with which he amused the whole crew suddenly stopped. He became wrapped in silence, and started staring intently in two directions – either southwards towards Asia Minor, or eastwards towards the Caucasus, although we were too far away at sea to be able to observe anything.

'What's the matter?' I asked. 'Are you regretting the fact that we're not sailing along the coast like the ancients?'

'You could say that,' muttered Misho. 'But not exactly. People often say that the ancients used coastal navigation, always keeping within sight of land. But Black Sea scholars have for a long time been debating the fact that experienced captains, who had circumnavigated the Black Sea shores enough times, might also have cut across some regions directly – as we were saying the other day about our crossing from Varna to Eregli, the direct route from Odessos to Heraclea Pontica. The only thing that worries me is how they managed to navigate without a compass or charts, especially when the weather was cloudy – the clouds cover up the stars at night, and in the day you can't tell the position of the sun.'

'Perhaps they knew the waves better – whether they are coming from the sea or the land.'

'That's another possibility. The trouble is that skills like that were forgotten with the advent of modern navigation systems, and now we'll have to rediscover them. And that's not easy at all, because this knowledge was accumulated on the basis of years of experience and observation of the tiniest details. Whereas today every fishing-smack has a compass and charts, not to mention radars, echo-sounders, satellite navigators . . .'

'But, even if we do set out without a compass and charts, we wouldn't be able to banish our modern knowledge of direction, coastlines and the geography of the region in general.'

'That's also true,' Misho agreed. 'And, on the other hand, we don't know how much of our modern knowledge was available to the ancients; so we have to be careful neither to overestimate nor to underestimate their abilities. And I think that that's the most difficult thing in any such experiment – to find the right balance.'

In the afternoon, Nature herself reminded us of one way of telling in which direction the coast lies. As we drifted there becalmed, we were suddenly invaded by swarms of flies, which evidently considered our cabins to be a convenient refuge and which ignored Yorrie's attempts to move them by attacking them with various sprays, whose only effect was to bring the entire crew out on deck. But, not before long, a few little birds flew down on to the spreaders, then boldly landed among us on the deck, and then started flying through the hatches in and out of the cabins as if they had spent all their lives on yachts like ours. They set upon the flies with gusto. When they had eaten their fill, they hopped out on deck to see us again and to rest after their meal. One of them landed on the compass, which was the only object on deck that always remained horizontal, shifted comfortably and left us a souvenir right in the middle of it. Having taken its bearings, it flew off, followed by the others. They flew exactly eastwards, which was where the nearest land – the coast of Georgia – was. This reminded Misho that in olden times sailors used to take cages of birds with them so that they could find the nearest coast.

In the meantime, the wind had started to blow again, in

different directions, until it finally settled on east-southeast. Blooper immediately started showing his worth, setting the Genoa jib and mainsail for sailing close-hauled, slackening and tightening the foresheet until there wasn't the slightest ripple in the sails; this showed that they were optimally adjusted. Petyo decided not to rely on the instinct of the birds, and took a few RDF bearings to find our precise location: we were 55 nautical miles from Poti.

During the night the wind dropped again, and Stoyan started doubting that we were near Georgia at all – if we were, where were the famous winds that blew down off the Caucasus? Henro ordered us to lower the sails and go to bed, leaving just one man on watch, in case the wind changed, or by chance another ship appeared. We doubted whether we would encounter another ship, since we were off any shipping lanes and, so far, had encountered just one other vessel.

We didn't reach Poti until the following afternoon. *Aurora* was immediately boarded by several members of the local committee which was to meet *Argo*.

'They must have informed you about our expedition in Tbilisi,' I enquired, as our letters had been sent to the organising committee in the Georgian capital.

'We haven't had any such information from Tbilisi,' they said, looking at each other, 'but we read about your expedition in *Pravda*, and so we were expecting you.'

Then Misho remembered that just before setting off from Varna he had been visited by the Bulgarian correspondent of *Pravda*, who had read about our expedition in the Bulgarian press. A little while later, they brought a copy of the paper with the article. According to *Pravda*, our meeting with the crew of *Argo* had already been arranged. All that remained for us to see now was whether Tim Severin knew about it, and when he would enter Soviet waters.

7

COLCHIS

'Kuchkhi bednieri! Kuchkhi bednieri!'

Only later did I find out that the Georgian for 'Welcome' literally meant 'lucky step'. As it happened, our first step on Georgian territory really was lucky, as we stepped straight into *Colchis*, the name of the sleek blue-and-white yacht beside which we tied up in Poti harbour. And, as luck would have it, the men aboard *Colchis* were the Georgian Argonauts – the men who would take over from the Turkish rowers when *Argo* entered Soviet waters. They reassured us that there were still four or five days to go before this happened, so there wasn't any hurry and – they insisted – we would spend our first evening as their guests aboard *Colchis*.

So, strictly speaking, we didn't actually step on Georgian soil that first evening. *Colchis*'s deck was strewn with an array of delicacies, whose names we did our best to remember: *khachapuri, satsiri, tkemali, khinkali* . . . No less 'aromatic' were the names of the wines we tasted: Tsinandali, Chkhavelli, Khvanchkara, Odjaleshi . . . Georgian speech flowed like song in the famous long-worded Georgian toasts. But Ilya Peradze outstripped all the others in this art. He was a huge Georgian who – raising a toast to the stepmother Ino, who had been the reason for Nephele's sending the golden-fleeced ram to save her children Phrixus and Helle – went on to enumerate all the main points of the myth of Jason and the Golden Fleece, and then proceeded to quote classical authors who had recounted the tale in so many different versions that now all we could do was wonder which was true and which was false – and all this was what had now brought us together on the deck of *Colchis* thirty-three centuries after Jason's expedition. *Gaumarjos!* Cheers!

The only attempt to respond in kind to this toast on our part was made by Henro, who raised his glass to the fact that we, after ordeals worthy of Jason himself and having set sail from Bulgaria with All Seas and Oceans visas, instead of heading off for the Pacific Ocean to try to solve the mystery of Easter Island, or crossing the Atlantic to rediscover America, had headed for none other than Poti because of Jason's uncle who had not wanted to cede the throne to him and so had sent him off on a wild-goose chase – i.e. the quest for the Golden Fleece, thus enabling us to end up aboard the yacht *Colchis* and, instead of wild goose, eat *khachapuri* and drink Tsinandali . . . *Gaumarjos!*

Over the next couple of days we were convinced that Tim Severin would also have a fairly trying time during his stay in Georgia. Because of the role of Jason he had adopted, the descendants of the Colchians had prepared a not inconsiderable number of ordeals for him, although they differed somewhat from the trials to which King Aeetes had subjected the Greek hero.

What actually had happened to Jason and the Argonauts in Colchis? When they reached the mouth of the river Phasis, they continued rowing upstream, finally stopping and hiding the ship in a bay overgrown with rushes. They were accompanied by four young men whom they had picked up *en route* on the isle of Ares. They were sons of Phrixus and had been on their way home to Orchomen from Colchis, when they were shipwrecked on Ares, and agreed to accompany the Argonauts back to Colchis to help them in their encounter with their grandfather Aeetes, king of the Colchians.

According to Apollonius, Jason held counsel with the Argonauts, who decided that he and two of their own number, together with the four grandsons of Aeetes, should go to the royal palace, state their intentions, and then he would decide what further course to take from the king's reaction. On the way to the palace the goddess Hera (or rather the riverside marshes) enveloped Jason and his company in a thick fog, thus enabling them to reach the very palace of Aeetes unnoticed. When they got there, the fog lifted. Through the eyes of his heroes, Apollonius gives us a marvellous description of the rich palace where Aetes lived together with his wife, their son Apsyrtus and their daughter Chalcyopes, wife of the deceased Phrixus, as well as Medea, the younger daughter, a sorceress and priestess in the temple of Hecate, who was to play an important role further on in the tale.

It was probably unnecessary for the goddesses Hera, Athena and Aphrodite, and Aphrodite's son Eros, to intervene at the crucial moment in the plot to help Jason get what he had come for; while Jason was talking with her father, Medea fell in love with the bold foreign traveller, and decided to help him. And Jason really needed assistance. When he told Aeetes what they had come for, his host flew into a rage and blamed the sons of Phrixus for the whole mess, believing that it was they who had brought the foreigners and were plotting together to overthrow him and become rulers of Colchis. It is interesting to see how Apollonius associates the Golden Fleece with the sceptre, symbol of royal power.

The political side of the story becomes even more marked when Jason assures the king that, if he is given the Golden Fleece, he will spread the word of Aeetes' glory throughout

Greece, and in addition offers him military assistance against the Sauromatae and other neighbouring tribes with whom Aeetes is warring.

It wouldn't be surprising if what Aeetes actually wanted was some kind of military alliance, because the ordeals through which he puts Jason can be interpreted as symbolising the defeat of enemy soldiers – the same ones that Aeetes himself had defeated earlier. What Aeetes had demanded of Jason was to plough a field dedicated to Ares, the god of war, with a plough harnessed to two copper-hooved, fire-breathing bulls, and to sow the fields with dragon's teeth, which turned into soldiers in armour, and to defeat them. Only then would he be allowed to take the Golden Fleece.

So Jason agreed and went back to *Argo* to tell the others what tasks Aeetes had set him. Then Argos, son of Phrixus, mentioned Medea's magical powers, which would be the only solution. Jason arranged to meet her in the temple of Hecate, and he too fell in love. Not that he had much choice – she was the only one who could save him. Medea gave him an ointment which would render him invulnerable and advised him how to fight the warriors; the next day Jason went out and succeeded in carrying out his tasks in the Field of Ares. Aeetes was displeased at the stranger's unusual strength, and called the elders of Colchis to a meeting to decide how they might foil the Argonauts. During that time, Medea secretly led Jason to the sacred forest of Ares and drugged the dragon that guarded the Golden Fleece on the sacred tree. Jason took the Golden Fleece and the two returned to *Argo*. Medea decided to flee together with Jason and his men.

When Aeetes heard what had happened, *Argo* was already far out to sea. The king of Colchis sent his own ships to follow *Argo* and recapture Medea . . .

A few days in the land of ancient Colchis were enough to

convince me that the intriguing story of the Golden Fleece is still very much alive among the Georgians. The tale is taught in schools, and it is also used in universities as a source for the study of Georgian history. Georgian scholars have made serious studies of all the different versions of *Argonautica*. For ordinary people the names of Jason and Medea are a part of their living folklore. Everyone is convinced that this was not just a myth or tale, but a real event which had been ornamented over thousands of years.

The inhabitants of Poti itself seemed to have the greatest grounds for curiosity. The actual name of the town can be regarded as a direct reference to the existence of trade between the Mycenaeans, i.e. the Greeks that lived at the time of Jason, and the Colchians. At one of our meetings in the Poti Interclub, I was told of this theory, which had been first put by Rismag Gordesiani, director of the Tbilisi Institute for Mediterranean Studies. The ancient Greeks called the river Rhioni, whose estuary is at Poti, the river Phasis. In the second half of the second millennium BC, which was when Jason's voyage took place, the people inhabiting Georgia spoke a language known as Kartvelian. According to Gordesiani, in that language the river would have been called Pati, which the Greeks would have transformed, according to the rules of their pronunciation, into Phasis. But some time around the end of the second millennium BC, Kartvelian disappeared as a language in western Georgia, and the people living along the river valley started speaking a language known as Mengrelian. In this language the name of the river was Poti, the same as the name of the town today. But the Greeks retained the original name of Phasis, which showed that they had learned it from before the late second millennium BC, i.e. a considerable time before the establishment of Greek trading settlements in Colchis during the final stage of the Great Colonisation.

Strabo, one of the most outstanding ancient geographers, also mentions Phasis. Strabo was born in the Pontian city of Amasia and his maternal uncle had been governor of Colchis when the ruler of the Pontian kingdom had been Mithridates VI. We can assume that Strabo, who himself was an enthusiastic traveller, had been to Colchis. He describes it in his *Geographia* as follows: 'By the river Phasis stands the city of the same name, emporium of the Colchians, who have the river on one side, the lake on the other and the sea on the third.'

We were taken to Lake Paliastomi near Poti, which is identified as the lake described by Strabo. At first sight it seemed obvious that this was the place where Phasis once stood, in the environs of the present-day town of Poti. But Gia Dardjania of the local *Argo* Reception Committee told me that changes in the course of the river Rhioni, and the spread of the land-mass due to the river's large deposits into the sea, made it difficult to determine the exact site of the city. Georgian archaeologists presume that the city had stood on a spot some six miles east of Poti. Indeed, preliminary archaeological and geological investigations show that the spot where Poti now stands and the area east of it were once occupied by a deep bay. Archaeological evidence of the Late Bronze Age, the period when King Aeetes and the Argonauts lived, can only be found from a point some 18 kilometres inland from Poti on the banks of the Rhioni.

In the works of some ancient authors, the capital of Aeetes is given the name of Aeae, and its site is indicated as being by the city of Phasis or on the river Phasis. It is even mentioned by Herodotus, the 'father of history', who we also assume travelled to Colchis at some point in his life. In his *Historia* he gives a summary of the Argonauts' exploits, and describes Aeae as being 'inland'. Other authors, including Apollonius Rhodius, call Aeetes' city Kutaia.

Misho Lazarov, who had visited Georgia several times already, and knew many of the local archaeologists personally, told me that some scholars identified Kutaia with the present town of Kutaisi, which is situated upstream on the river Phasis. Our hosts from Poti were waiting for just that – the moment we mentioned an interest in the ancient Colchian city, they arranged a visit to it.

As we travelled towards Kutaisi in a minibus, Misho and I looked at a map of Georgia. I wanted to see how far ancient Colchis had extended, at least in the minds of ancient geographers. It had covered the whole of the Western Caucasus down to the Black Sea. In the east, its boundary was the Likhsky Ridge, which links the Great and Little Caucasus; northwards it reached to the Great Caucasus; and southwards to the Meskhetsky Ridge of the Little Caucasus.

'Of course, they weren't permanent boundaries,' said Lazarov, 'because over the centuries Colchis grew and shrunk, sometimes being larger and sometimes smaller than the main regions inhabited by Colchian tribes.'

Excavations in Kutaisi and its environs have revealed the importance of this region, divulging numerous sites ranging from the late Bronze and early Iron Ages to the classical age. At the local Ethnographical and History Museum, an important centre for Georgian studies, we saw some of the finds. They included bronze figures of bulls and stone engravings of bull's heads, or Minotaurs, which were evidence of a bull cult in ancient Colchis. Might it have some connection with Jason's ordeal with the two wild bulls? Perhaps those who compiled the myths of Jason and the Golden Fleece saw a relation between the bull cult and taming the bulls and the acquisition of the Golden Fleece – or, according to one version, the acquisition of royal power.

The museum also had figures of snakes, although one of our hosts from Kutaisi told us that there had been no serpent cult

THE ARGONAUTICA EXPEDITION

... Nevertheless, in the mythology of the Colchians, as indeed of the Thracians, the snake was the guardian of the hearth. It was also supposed that the temples of the ancient Colchians had guardian serpents. And if there really had been a Golden Fleece, regardless of whether it had been a symbol or not, where else would it have been kept other than in a well-guarded temple?

As I stared at the pictures of bulls and snakes, Misho Lazarov, whom I was constantly pestering with my questions and queries, had rushed ahead until he reached one particular hall, where he stopped and waited for us to come and see what he was looking at. With a theatrical gesture he drew our attention to one exhibit in a corner. It was a huge piece of stone, rounded to an approximate pear shape, with a hole in its top part.

'A stone anchor?' Sergei asked in surprise.

'It most certainly is!' said Misho, rubbing his hands in satisfaction. 'And whenever I ask my Soviet colleagues about stone anchors – they know I have a bee in my bonnet about stone anchors – they keep telling me they haven't discovered any stone anchors along their part of the coast. But, as you can see, the Georgians do have them. And do you know what this particular anchor reminds me of? The ancient geographer Arianus once travelled around the coast of the Black Sea to make a report on it for the emperor Hadrian. This report actually formed the basis of his geographical essay *Periplus ad Pontos Euxeinos*. Arianus describes how, reaching the mouth of the Phasis where, according to the legend, the Argonauts landed, they showed him anchors reputed to be from the original *Argo*. The geographer says that one of them, an iron anchor, did not seem to him to be very old, although it was different in size and shape from contemporary anchors. But they showed him the remains of a stone anchor which could really be considered the remains of *Argo*'s anchor. What's

COLCHIS

important to me isn't so much Arianus's interest in *Argo* herself; he was an educated man and he probably knew everything about Jason's voyage in the Black Sea, and all the other Greek myths. But his remark that the Argonauts used a stone anchor on their voyage to Colchis is probably the key to the riddle of the first entry by ships of the Mediterranean into the Black Sea.'

'You go looking all over the place, and wherever you go you end up with stone anchors!' laughed Henro, listening to Misho.

'Naturally. Navigation is an element of a developed maritime culture. And the Black Sea cultures reached their second height in the middle and the second half of the second millennium BC, or the Late Bronze Age, which was when the Argonauts lived. The most devel̈oped centres were the western and eastern Black Sea, in other words, the Thracian and Colchian civilisations. At this time, the Cretan and Mycenaean civilisations flourished in the eastern Mediterranean. And this is what makes Arianus's points so interesting: first, that there were ancient anchors to be found in the eastern part of the Black Sea, and, second, that he immediately associates them with the Argonauts.

'Apart from the anchors, is there any other evidence of a developed maritime culture among the Colchians?' asked Petyo, for whom one answer was usually not enough.

'If we believe the myth of the Argonauts,' I put in, 'the Colchians had faster ships than *Argo*, or perhaps it was simply that they knew the waters better. When Apsyrtus is sent by his father Aeetes to chase the Argonauts after they make off with Medea and the Golden Fleece, he manages to outstrip *Argo* and seal off the routes by which the Argonauts might return: the Bosphorus, the Danube, and in some versions even the Adriatic Sea. The ancients believed that the Istros, or Danube, was linked to the Adriatic by a separate channel which allowed ships to get back along it to the Aegean via the Ionian Sea.'

123

'But was it possible for them to have sailed on such long stretches without charts?' Petyo asked. 'I can't imagine how they'd have done it in those days without any navigating equipment.'

'The *Kirbes!*' said our guides in the museum. 'Apollonius and his ancient commentators also found it difficult to believe that someone could sail such vast distances without charts, because at that time a primitive form of charts already existed. Apollonius believed that the Colchians possessed something similar – he mentions that they possessed notes passed down to them from their forefathers and written on *kirbi*, which showed seafarers all the routes and coastlines. They're also mentioned by other Greek writers, some of whom believed that they were the earliest form of stone, copper and terracotta tablets used to record a wide variety of information.'

'I've got a friend from Leningrad,' Misho added, 'Alexander Slisarenko, who also studies navigation in ancient times. In one of his books he devotes a whole chapter to the Argonauts. Anyway, he once told me that the earliest surviving chart of the Black Sea is one compiled by the Roman admiral Agrippa. There must have been some earlier prototypes which he used to get his information, because it's all very accurate and can't have been based just on stories.'

'Another curious piece of information is that the ancient people inhabiting the Black Sea knew their bits of coastline,' said one of our hosts from Kutaisi. 'It comes from Lucius Septimius, who says that at the time before the Greeks knew their way around in the Black Sea they hired local pilots, "barbarians" they called them, to guide them. So obviously the history of local navigation pre-dated the coming of the Greeks.'

Petyo had got answers to many of his questions, but I was still eager to find out what we had actually come here to learn

COLCHIS

– the connection between this ancient city and between Aeae, capital of Aeetes' kingdom.

In the museum we were able to familiarise ourselves with the studies of the Georgian historian Muskhelishvili. He supported those scholars who claimed that the Colchian city of Kutaia, mentioned in ancient literature in connection with the Argonaut myth, was the same as the later Kutaisi. One of the pieces of evidence they used to support this claim was the writings of the Byzantine historian Procopius Caesarius, who wrote:

> Through this country flows a river by the name of Rhioni, where in ancient times the Colchians had built a fort . . . In Greek this fort was known as Kotiaion, while today the Lazars call it Kutaisom, their ignorance of Greek causing them to change the pronunciation. Thus Arianus explains it in his history. Others say that in ancient times there stood here a city named Koitaios. This was where Aeetes was from, and that was why the poets call it Koitai, and Colchis itself Koitaida.

Our hosts from Kutaisi didn't want us to think them guilty of local patriotism, and so they left us to draw our own conclusions, although they didn't fail to mention that in the Middle Ages, too, their city had been a political centre of the Western Georgian and afterwards of the Georgian kingdom for a certain time. After the disintegration of the single feudal monarchy, Kutaisi became capital of the Imeritian kingdom.

When we returned to Poti, our conception of King Aeetes' capital became confused. According to the people of Poti, who also referred to ancient sources, this capital had been situated in a convenient bay at the mouth of the river Phasis. Thus they identified the ancient city of Aeae with the as yet undiscovered city of Phasis near Poti. I didn't want to argue with the people of Poti, geared up as they were over the coming arrival of *Argo*, but to me the most likely answer seemed to be that Phasis would have developed as the principal Colchian trading centre thanks to its position both on a river and on the sea, while Kutaia, or Kutaisi, had been the political centre and Aeetes' place of residence, deliberately situated inland to make it more immune to sudden invasion by sea.

In the end, Misho Lazarov found the best solution, which he based on the authority of Professor Othar Lordkipanidze, director of the Archaeological Studies Centre of the Georgian Academy of Sciences. He was expected to arrive in Poti at the head of a team of archaeologists and historians to receive *Argo* and Tim Severin. Misho had met Professor Lordkipanidze several times before, and now told us his colleague's view that in the earliest sources Aeae was mentioned as the name of the whole country, while only in later writings is it used to denote just the city, with the location of the city being described differently – sometimes it is near the city of Phasis, while at other times it is on the river Phasis.

In Poti, preparations for the reception of *Argo* were in full swing. The dozen or so rowers from our neighbour, *Colchis*, who were soon to join the Argonauts, trained every day by rowing a boat with extra-heavy oars upstream along the river Rhioni. Among these robust men was a shorter one, albeit just as muscular and energetic. He was Paatha Natsvlishvili, president of the Young Georgian Journalists' Union. All the rest were Masters of Sport in rowing and they came from different Georgian cities, although half of them were locals from Poti. Like Tim Severin's Argonauts, they too were an international team – apart from Georgians, they included some Russians living in Batumi, a Lithuanian from Poti, and a Greek from Tbilisi. Georgia was, in fact, one of the Soviet republics with the largest number of nationalities. Paatha had become one of the rowing team when a Georgian newspaper had asked him to write an article about *Argo*'s visit, and had been asked what he would require to help him to do so.

'To become one of the Argonauts!' had been Paatha's reply, and he promptly set about training to row so that he would be up to the level of all the others.

I got on well with him. After all, apart from our common interest in history, Tim Severin and the Jason Voyage, we were also fellow journalists. Paatha promised to introduce me to all the more interesting people who were coming to Poti for *Argo*'s reception.

The first was actually someone who had come down specially to see us after reading about our expedition in *Pravda*. Valery Chaprava was from the town of Meore Gudava in Abkhazia which, he told us, had been founded by the Greeks, who had called it Siganeon. Valery was one of those magnificent people who can devote years of their lives to solving some riddle without expecting any reward for themselves in the form of titles or even recognition. Fascinated by the myth of Jason and the Argonauts, he had spent nigh on twenty years gleaning pieces of information from ancient authors on the subject scrap by scrap. And he did it all simply for the fun of it, and not to seek sudden fame as the originator of a new hypothesis.

'Is there anything new to think up?' he smiled, producing from his bag several thick notebooks and folders and starting to look through one of them, pleased to be able to speak to people with like interests instead of people who listened to him as if he were some kind of crank. 'The ancient writers have left so many different versions of the story anyway. Look at this, for example!' he exclaimed, opening his file at a page which had written in large letters at the top the name 'Palephates' and opposite it, '4th Century BC' and a big question mark beside it. 'The quotation I shall read you now is from an anonymous mythographical treatise of the second century, although it is supposed to originate from Palephates: "What the Colchians had guarded was not in fact a golden fleece, but a book written on animal hides describing the way in which gold could be obtained by chemical methods." Interesting, isn't it? Two thousand years ago people were already wondering about this. Or take Charaxus of Pergamon, second to third centuries. His words were preserved by the Byzantine commentator Eustace of Salonika: "The Golden Fleece was a way of writing in gold on parchment and they say that that was the reason for *Argo*'s voyage." And here I have the famous opinion of Strabo, who to this day remains one of the most popular versions of the reasons for Jason's exploits: "There are also many tales in existence of this country's wealth, consisting of gold, silver and iron, which allow us to guess what the real reason for the expedition, and for Phrixus's previous expedition, had been. There are also monuments to the two expeditions: to Phrixus on the border between Colchis and Iberia, and to Jason." Later on, in his *Terralogia*, Pomponius Mela also mentions a temple to Phrixus in Colchis. These are the more widely known viewpoints, but I've collected a lot of other details. I'll try to speak with Tim Severin to see if I can help him in any way.'

I for my part thought it hardly possible that any more versions of the tale of the Golden Fleece could exist, but my fellow journalists from the Soviet magazine *Vokrug Sveta* managed to surprise me there. Their chief editor, Alexander Poleshchuk, who had some months earlier informed me about the coming arrival of Tim Severin in Georgia, had kept his promise to send along his colleague from the international department, Vitaly Babenko, to Poti before *Argo*'s arrival so that we'd have time to compare notes. Vitaly, although young, had travelled widely and seen a lot of things, and so was not one of those people who would wildly applaud any hypothesis that was presented with enough imagination. He simply set out the

COLCHIS

arguments for another possible reason for the Argonauts' voyage which *Vokrug Sveta* intended to publish. The hypothesis had come from the chemist Igor Mashnikov. He based it on the idea that, according to Herodotus, Strabo and others, the flax that had once grown in Greece had been of fairly bad quality and produced only rough fabric, causing the Hellenes to resort to imports from Egypt. But, as Colchis exported the best-quality flax of all the countries of the ancient East, why should they not have traded with Greece? Most scholars see the myth of Jason and the Argonauts as evidence of trading contacts between the Greeks and the Colchians. But why would the ancient Greeks travel such a great distance just to get the sheepskins the Colchians used to gather gold with? Mashnikov believed that the Golden Fleece might not have been a sheepskin, and had nothing to do with gold at all. What, then, was it? By looking closely at the operations involved in gathering gold from Georgian rivers using sheepskins as described by ancient authors, he focused on the detail that the skin had to be left submerged in the water for two days. Why only two? The longer you leave a sheepskin in the water, the greater the quantity of gold that will gather in the fibres of the wool. According to Mashnikov, this method was rather reminiscent of the earliest method of steeping flax. It is here that the period of soaking is of paramount importance, and if it is soaked for too long the quality of the fibre deteriorates. Mashnikov went on to say that during the time of the Trojan War – i.e. about the time of the Argonauts – the best-quality linen was valued several times higher than gold in Greece. This brought him to the conclusion that the Golden Fleece might actually have been the finest linen. But, it being unlikely that the Greeks would have undertaken such a perilous expedition just for a shipload – or possibly even several shiploads – of fine linen, Mashnikov then turned to the special role played by Medea in the myth. She was a priestess in the temple of Hecate, and in the ancient world the priests and priestesses were those who guarded the secrets that were of any value to their country. Thus Mashnikov concludes that the abduction of Medea, who was keeper of the secret of obtaining good-quality linen, had been the main purpose of the Argonauts' expedition to Colchis.

There is possibly a grain of truth in this romantic and chemical interpretation. After all, the abduction of the beautiful Helen had ostensibly been the cause of the Trojan War, which had led to the birth of Homer's epic, the *Iliad*. Still, Vitaly Babenko preferred to see Medea not so much as the keeper of the secret of high-quality linen but rather as an expert in the medical properties of the herbs for which the Colchians were famed in the ancient world. Vitaly told me that the German scholar Sprengel mentions thirty-six plants that grow only in Colchis in his five-volume history of medicine. Almost all of these herbs are also mentioned in the *Orphic Argonautica*, which contains a detailed description of the different magical herbs growing in the garden of Hecate on the banks of the Phasis. And Medea was high priestess of Hecate.

When Babenko mentioned the *Orphic Argonautica*, it occurred to me that in the fuss surrounding *Argo*'s arrival I wouldn't have much chance to talk to the Georgian scholars about the extent to which the figure of Orpheus is retained in Colchian memory. Nikola Gigov had requested me to do this on our trip to the Rhodopes, as he himself would be in the Mediterranean in July and didn't think he would manage to come to Georgia straight after that.

But now, two or three days after *Argo* had entered Soviet waters, as Misho and I were passing the time of day chatting in *Aurora*'s cockpit, I heard someone greet us in Georgian from the quayside.

'*Gamarjoba!*' And then, in Bulgarian, 'How're the Argonauts?'

I recognised the voice. I jumped up and looked over towards the quay. There was Nikola Gigov, his arm raised in greeting. It turned out that he'd had a stroke of good luck and managed to sort out the formalities for a trip to Georgia in just a few days after his return from the Mediterranean.

Nikola was dying to talk with Georgian historians on his pet subject. Our hospitable colleagues from the local newspaper *New Colchis* for their part were also dying to help him as soon as possible, and so he was immediately carted off to the ancient city of Archeolopolis to meet a number of professors. Old Georgian tradition cites the town of Tsikha-Goji as the main city of Colchis. This town is identified with the city of Archeopolis mentioned by Byzantine chroniclers, which is situated on the banks of the river Tekhuri, and coincides with the present-day city of Nokalakevi. Archaeological excavations there have brought to light evidence of the Hellenic period.

In Archeopolis Nikola had met the professors Lekvinadze, Zakaria and Lomouri.

'I asked them about Orpheus, of course,' he said on his return, leafing through his notebook. 'Professor Lomouri told me that Dionysus is more commonplace here than Orpheus. The Georgian cult of Dionysus and wine has overshadowed the cult of the Thracian bard. Lomouri told me that because of Byzantine writings Dionysus and Orpheus were associated with Greek mythology. No one has made a really thorough analysis of the national composition of the Argonauts. And that's such an interesting subject! They told me that in Phasis there had been a temple of Apollo, and I told them my view that the temples of Apollo were a Greek version of the cult of Orpheus. And the Greeks agree that this is true even of their main shrine in Delphi.'

'Didn't they tell you where you might eventually be able to find any connection with the image of Orpheus?' I asked.

'They mentioned several Georgian books, published by Tsereteli, containing the findings of the German archaeologist Schneider who did some research here. They also told me to look for images of Orpheus on the engraved gems that have been discovered. Incidentally, on my way back from Archeopolis, I spent several hours in the local history museum at Poti and stumbled across an anonymous depiction of *Argo*, with Jason standing on the prow, and Orpheus beside him with his lyre.'

I showed Nikola the wooden carving symbolising the art of Orpheus which Rangel had made for our meeting with the new *Argo*.

'He certainly knows what Orpheus is all about!' exclaimed Nikola. 'You must introduce him to me when we get back. If Tim Severin can understand the symbolism, he'll definitely like it! Actually, when is *Argo* due here? Have you heard anything new?'

The next day there was a great deal of bustling aboard *Colchis*. They had been advised to set sail for Batumi, and from there proceed towards the Turkish border where they should wait for *Argo*. When we heard this, panic ensued on our yacht. In their kind enthusiasm to show us as much as possible, our hosts from Poti had forgotten the most important thing of all, which was to repair our engine. Without it Henro didn't want to risk setting sail. On the very first day one of the young men who had greeted us had promised to fashion another part for us, but since then we hadn't heard from him. Henro started getting impatient, and despatched Petyo and Sergei to find Zaza – that was the young man's name – and not to come back without the new part. At several points during the day we saw Sergei appear on the quay, not daring to get aboard the yacht, fuming in despair when we told him that Zaza hadn't come yet. 'Where the hell has that Zaza got himself to?' he barked. Then Moscow came to our assistance. Yakov Kaganov and Vitaly Dorozhinksi of *Turist* magazine were eager to accompany us on *Aurora*, and so joined the search-party for Zaza, enlisting all their local acquaintances too.

After a great deal of rushing about on the part of Petyo, Sergei, Yakov and Vitaly – evil tongues say that they conducted the bulk of their search from the pleasant café beneath the tower in the town centre – Zaza appeared on the quayside just when we had abandoned all hope of ever seeing him again in our lives. We smiled pleasantly at him, as if he'd just gone off to repair the part half an hour earlier, and not a week ago, and he, with the air of one who has done a good job, solemnly presented us with the piece of iron wrapped in oily paper as if it were the Golden Fleece itself. It was late evening, and there was no time to start installing the part now, so nothing remained for us to do other than bring out some of our rather diminished supplies of 'liquid gold' and thank Zaza for the prompt service he had rendered us.

At daybreak Stoyan, Petyo and Henro managed to get the new part installed, and to Zaza's enthusiastic waves and shouts of 'Good luck!' we chugged out of Poti harbour and raised the sails, heading southwards in the direction from which *Argo* was to appear.

8

MEETING *ARGO*

Maltakva, Grigoleti, Ureki, Kvemo-Natanebi, Kobuleti . . . Village after village with exotic-sounding names appeared to port on the flat Georgian coastline between Poti and Batumi. In normal conditions we would probably have tried to sail in as close as possible to them, and even stop off to see what lay behind these mysterious names. To me they sounded like the names of some ancient Georgian clans that lined the shores in national costumes, waiting in silent dignity to greet the modern Argonauts.

'*Gamarjoba*, Grigoleti! *Gamarjoba*, Ureki!' we shouted in greeting from *Aurora* as the sails flapped when we changed tack, which we had to do often. We were sailing upwind close-hauled, heading towards the coast on one tack, then going about and heading out into the open sea on the other, leaving the next village behind us. 'Goodbye, Kvemo-Natanebi! Hope to see you some other time!'

We had to hurry, because the wind was in *Argo*'s favour, and we had no idea how much progress Tim Severin had made. And if we didn't manage to sight *Argo* while it was still light, there was the danger of missing her at night, because with lights she wouldn't look any different from a large fishing-boat.

MEETING ARGO

At about noon the sun broke through the sea-mist, which now hung in rags around the yacht. The grey metallic colour of the water changed to pale green, which meant that there were shallows about. As a precaution, Henro moved us further away from shore, and continued on longer tacks towards the open sea, to the evident relief of Yakov and Vitaly, whose stomachs had obviously not taken very kindly to the frequent about-turns. Sergei immediately set about caring for his compatriots. To raise their spirits, he told them the spiciest sailors' jokes he knew, which were enough to make you feel sick even if you had the strongest stomach on the entire Black Sea. Then he decided that this wasn't enough, so he cooked up yet another version of *azu*, this time *à la Georgian*, naturally, by mixing all the vegetables we'd managed to buy in Poti and adding generous quantities of Tsinandali – 'to get their spirits up', as he said. After the first few mouthfuls Yakov and Vitaly tactfully announced that they were not yet accustomed to Georgian cuisine. But they did throw themselves eagerly upon the Bulgarian sheep's cheese we produced, which is a food worthy of any ancient mariner.

It started to rain in the early afternoon, and after Kobuleti we again entered ragged mist. We all fell silent and stared towards the coast, supposing that *Argo*, which lay less than a metre in the water, would be hugging the sandy coastline.

Suddenly the short-wave radio crackled. Henro had left it on stand-by, as he had agreed to keep contact with the captain of *Colchis* on the day that *Argo* was expected. I leaped over to the navigator's desk and turned up the volume. The radio boomed out in English:

'*Argo, Argo*, do you read me? This is *Tovarishch* . . .'

I called Henro over, as the voice continued to repeat:

'*Argo, Argo*, do you read me? This is *Tovarishch* . . .'

Henro looked at me.

135

'Well, that can only mean one thing. They're somewhere in the vicinity. You remember yesterday, what Ilya said when *Colchis* set off? He said that *Tovarishch* was going to join them and they'd meet up with *Argo* together.'

We jumped out on deck and got out our binoculars. Sergei even produced a telescope from somewhere – he had been saving it specially for this moment, so that he'd be the first to see *Argo*. But nothing could be seen through the mist, while all the time the radio-set continued to make noises. Then came a second voice, this time in proper English:

'*Tovarishch*, this is *Argo*. I read you loud and clear.'

Sergei leaped up and excitedly rushed to the navigator's cockpit:

'Did you hear that? It was *Argo*. Let's call them up too! They must be somewhere near!'

'Calm down a bit, will you,' Henro reprimanded him, raising his binoculars again. 'Let's see first, and then let them see us, then we'll have time for a chat.'

Argo continued to broadcast her message to *Tovarishch*:

'Richard and John are on their way over in the dinghy. Do you read me? Reading you loud and clear . . .'

'We read you loud and clear. We are expecting the dinghy. Leave your radio on stand-by, channel 14 . . .'

Again Sergei couldn't keep still:

'They're near, they're near . . . They must be, if they're sending a dinghy over . . .'

And soon afterwards we noticed three thin vertical lines on the horizon. When they grew bigger, they turned into the masts of *Tovarishch*, the famous Soviet training barquentine, one of the fastest sailing-ships afloat. Yakov told us that the ship had been built in 1933 in Hamburg and had been christened *Gork Fock*. She had sunk, and in 1946 Soviet sailors had salvaged her, repaired her and given her to the Kherson naval school. Ilya

MEETING ARGO

Peradze had told Henro that aboard *Tovarishch* there should be a group of Georgian archaeologists and historians led by Othar Lordkipanidze, as well as some journalists led by the doctor Yuri Senkevich, who had taken part in Thor Heyerdahl's Ra and Tigris Expeditions. Yuri Senkevich was now the presenter of one of the most popular Soviet TV programmes, called *Travellers' Club*.

Other masts appeared on the horizon beside *Tovarishch*. One we recognised as *Colchis*, and probably others had come out from Batumi to meet up with *Argo*. But where was the galley itself?

I stood in the bow of *Aurora*, my eye glued to the telescope, which Sergei had generously given up to me, although his eagerness to sight *Argo* was as great as mine. I noticed that *Tovarishch* was moving under just a single sail on the bowsprit. That meant it was deliberately keeping to a low speed to wait for someone.

The chill head wind made my eyes water, while the leaden clouds rushed across the metallic green sea. I rubbed my eyes and then peered into the telescope again. Where was *Argo*?

Then Henro took the yacht about. *Aurora* crossed *Tovarishch*'s path, and we were now to starboard of the impressive sailing-vessel, but still about two miles distant.

Then I spotted *Argo*. She was instantly recognisable by her unusual rectangular sail. She was sailing immediately to starboard of *Tovarishch*, which was why we hadn't seen her until then. Henro steered *Aurora* towards the galley. Slowly, the details of the craft came into view. On her sails were painted three Greek warriors with spears and shields on which were depicted ram's heads – the coat of arms of the Aeolids, Jason's family. *Argo*'s hull to some extent resembled that of one of our *maunas*, traditional fishing and cargo boats. It had retained the natural colour of its wood. It was only partially painted with a blue wavy line on a white background in the places where the fore and aft bridges of a *mauna* should be. The bow had a long ram which had also been painted to resemble a dolphin's head – an ancient tradition which can still be seen on boats in the Mediterranean today, and even in Bulgaria. The stern was raised and curved inwards. In fact, it had been built to look just like the galleys depicted on ancient Greek vases.

There were no oars to be seen on *Argo*. They had probably shipped the oars and were relying wholly on the wind, since the single sail, which hung from a wooden beam attached about one yard below the top of the mast, was billowing in the wind, making the three Mycenaean warriors move as if they, and not the galley, were advancing towards Colchis in search of the Golden Fleece.

When we got within twenty yards of *Argo*, I realised that the man on deck who was steering the ship using the two steering-oars was not Tim Severin, whose face I knew from the books I had read. We waved to the crew, and were answered by loud cheers. After almost three months of rowing all the way from Volos to the shores of Colchis, every meeting with fellow mariners must have added some variety to the lives of the modern Argonauts. I was still trying to see which one of the men on board was Tim Severin when Paatha stood up from one of the rowing-benches and shouted to us that some of the crew, including Tim Severin, had gone over to *Tovarishch*, where a sort of press-conference was just being held.

'What's it like on *Argo*?' I asked Paatha.

'We are unlucky!' he replied in English, so that the rest of the rowers would understand. 'Since this morning there's been a fair wind blowing, and we haven't had the chance to row yet. We've just been sailing all the time. Very unpleasant!'

At which, of course, all of Tim Severin's men burst into laughter. They had been aboard almost eighty days since they set out, almost constantly struggling against headwinds, relying only on their oars. One of the crew had even calculated that to get here had taken them about one and a half million oar-strokes! So every opportunity to proceed under sail and to rest their muscles a while was to them like a blessing from the god Aeolus himself.

But the enthusiastic Georgians, whose leader was a champion of the Soviet Spartakiad, were itching to show what they were made of. After so much training, it really was bad luck for them that on their first day *Argo* should be sailing in a fair wind while they had to sit there like tourists.

Paatha exchanged a few words with one of the British crew beside him, who also stood up:

'I hear you've come all the way from the western coast of the Black Sea, from Bulgaria. Are people interested in the Golden Fleece there?'

I told him of our expedition, and the studies made by Bulgarian archaeologists and historians which we had translated into English for Tim Severin, and also about our gold ingot.

'Fantastic!' he said, laughing. 'So it's been worth coming all this way to find the Golden Fleece. When Tim gets back, we'll tell him there's no need to go on, then, if you know where the Fleece is.'

Soon afterwards the radio again spoke up. *Tovarishch* was calling *Argo* to send her inflatable dinghy across to pick up Tim Severin and some of his Argonauts. The dinghy puttered across to *Tovarishch*.

Among us, the tension grew. Although the distance between *Tovarishch* and ourselves and *Argo* had increased, it wouldn't take the dinghy more than quarter of an hour to pick up Tim Severin and bring him back. The moment of our first meeting was drawing near. Sergei was growing more and more impatient by the minute. Where was Tim Severin's dinghy? Why was it taking its time? Had something happened to it in the swell? Had the outboard engine broken down? Perhaps we should go and look for it in our dinghy . . . Henro listened to him in silence. He hated being pressurised into making hasty decisions.

'Come on, let's go and take a look, see how the land lies!' insisted Sergei.

Henro got up slowly, but instead of going towards our inflatable he headed towards the stern.

'Hang on, I'm just going to take a leak, otherwise . . .'

'Very good, very good,' Sergei said, nodding his approval. 'Otherwise it'll go to your head . . . You won't be able to think quickly . . .'

Misho laughed loudly at this, but it was no longer necessary to undertake anything, because *Argo*'s dinghy had appeared. I raised my telescope again. Among the four men in the boat was someone who was their senior, with a beard and a brick-red peaked cap on his head. I recognised the cap from photos of Tim Severin that I had seen in Greek newspapers taken on the *Argo*'s departure from Volos. That had to be him!

Our yacht had lagged behind *Argo*, and now the dinghy would have to pass us. As I tried to think up the most suitable words with which to greet Tim Severin, the outboard roared up to starboard. Tim raised his hand in greeting, then pointed first to his ear and then towards the outboard engine. In all the excitement I'd forgotten that, however loudly I expressed my great pleasure at meeting him, the noise of the outboard would drown out my words. The dinghy drew up beside *Argo*, and when Tim had boarded the galley, the other man I had spoken to said something, pointing in our direction. Tim smiled at us, and motioned us to draw closer – he preferred to speak from board to board. He called:

'Are you Troev? I got your letters, they were forwarded to

me from London. I'm glad you managed to organise everything to come and meet us here.'

I suddenly felt a great relief. All the time I'd been worrying how to explain everything I'd written in my letters to Tim Severin as briefly as possible: the aim of our expedition and its connection with the Jason Voyage.

'Nice yacht!' Tim went on, looking carefully at *Aurora*. 'I love wooden yachts. Classic stuff!'

I glanced at Henro, who was at the helm. His face beamed with pleasure, and he answered:

'And *Argo* looks like a pretty sound smack, if she's lasted all this way...'

'Want to swap?' the helmsman shouted over, and the other Argonauts all laughed. Obviously standing upright for hours at *Argo*'s steering-oars wasn't as relaxing as steering our yacht looked from the outside: Henro was sitting comfortably on the cushioned seat behind the wheel and was elegantly steering the obedient *Aurora* with one hand.

Imperceptibly, evening was coming, and I asked Tim when we'd have time to see each other and have a talk.

'We're going to try to use the favourable wind to get as near to Poti as possible now, and probably anchor for the night near Grigoleti, as the Georgians have advised us. Then, if the weather's OK I'll come aboard your yacht, and, if not, we'll see each other tomorrow morning on the way to Poti.'

'OK then, we'll keep as close to *Argo* as possible this evening,' I confirmed. 'And, just in case, we'll keep our radio on channel 14, as your wireless operator told us.'

'Remember that our transmitter batteries are almost flat,' shouted Tim. 'So we mightn't be able to call you. But we'll see you tomorrow at the latest. Watch out along this shore at night, I've heard that there are sandbanks!'

It grew pitch dark, and *Argo*'s light at the top of her mast was turned on. If we had passed her at night, we would have had great difficulty in distinguishing the galley from any other boat. The moon had vanished behind the clouds and the stars, so all that could be seen of *Argo* at night was the dimly glowing light at the top of the mast to warn passing ships that something was sailing there in the dark.

Suddenly lightning flashed in the blackened sky, throwing the silhouette of the galley into focus. The effect was unforgettable. As we peered into the darkness trying to distinguish *Argo*, the lightning would suddenly show us the shape of the galley somewhere farther ahead than we had expected. Then we would have the after-image of the galley in the darkness for a few seconds, until another flash of lightning made it appear farther ahead. *Argo* seemed to be travelling in time, jumping through the millennia with every flash of lightning to merge again with its legendary predecessor. And it all happened in some kind of eerie silence – there were no claps of thunder after the flashes of lightning, while the crash of the breaking waves had started to change into a peculiar hissing.

'I don't like the sound of those hissing waves!' said Henro, jerking me out of my trance. 'They sound like shallows to me, and if *Argo*'s draught is only half a metre Tim doesn't have to worry about where to go, but, if we get grounded, then we've had it! Look at the other yachts – they're far out at sea, and some have gone ahead to Poti.'

'Well, you head out a little, and I'll try to make contact with *Argo* to see what their intentions are.'

The Argonauts probably heard me when I called them on the short-wave radio, but they didn't answer. Their battery was probably flat, as Tim had warned. Then they flashed a spotlight at us a few times, and then illuminated the sail, which was just being lowered. They had decided to anchor for the night. For an instant the towering shadow of Tim Severin showed up against the sail, and then everything went dark, after which a hurricane lamp was lit on the stern. They were probably going to put in for the night.

The lights of the other yachts were no longer to be seen, and *Tovarishch* had long pulled out to sea to keep clear of the shallows. Henro got in touch with *Colchis* over the radio and found out that all had retired to Poti to anchor in the harbour and would sail out to join *Argo* again in the morning.

'There's nothing we can do out here all night,' Henro decided. 'Obviously everything's all right aboard the galley if they're not giving any distress signals. Let's hoist the mainsail and get back to Poti. Zaza's probably waiting for us there, and I'm beginning to miss seeing his face . . .'

We got back into Poti around midnight, after the other yachts had all finished celebrating their first encounter with *Argo*. But in the morning we were the first out. Again the coast was shrouded in mist, but we already knew where to look for the galley, and made for Grigoleti. As we approached the town, we could make out *Tovarishch's* silhouette in the distance, and then *Argo's* square sail between the three-master and the shore.

The galley had set out at first light to use as much as possible of the wind, which was now dying down. In the meantime, Yuri Senkevich had managed to call Tim Severin aboard *Tovarishch* to discuss their programme for the arrival in Poti.

Soon the wind had died down completely, and the Georgian rowers could finally have the pleasure of manning the oars.

Misho Lazarov paced *Aurora's* deck and watched the galley with interest.

'It looks rather like a *mauna* to me,' he suggested tentatively. 'Actually, that might not be the best comparison, but they remind me of the boats, which came in different sizes, which Bulgarian sailors once used to sail around the Black Sea and all the way to the eastern Mediterranean, just a few decades ago.

It's strange the way tradition sticks. We must ask Tim Severin about that Greek shipwright and how he built it.'

We had many more questions we wanted to ask Tim Severin, but he was taking his time aboard *Tovarishch*, and when his dinghy roared past us on its way back to *Argo* the other yachts from Poti had also arrived and were rocking around the galley. Everyone wanted to get as close to it as possible. Finally *Colchis*, which was their flagship, managed to get some kind of order, giving each craft its own special position in the guard of honour that was to accompany *Argo* into Poti. *Aurora* was positioned right after *Colchis*, and at one point we happened to be alongside *Argo*, with some twenty metres of water between us.

We decided to take this opportunity, since we would hardly have a peaceful moment in the tumultuous reception that awaited Tim Severin in Poti. At the same time, Yuri Senkevich boarded *Argo*. It was time to get the Soviet passengers of *Aurora* into action. I nodded to Yakov, who knew Yuri Senkevich personally, and he called out to ask him whether this was a convenient time for us to board *Argo*. Yuri spoke to Tim Severin, who immmediately turned and waved to us:

'Come on, Theodor! The dinghy's coming right now . . .'

My breath stopped. The moment I had been awaiting for so long had arrived, and suddenly I felt unprepared, although I'd gone over the meeting in my mind at least a dozen times beforehand. I scrambled below deck and picked up the wooden Orpheus figurine, dragged out the folder containing the findings of Bulgarian archaeologists and historians, translated into English for Tim . . . And as I wondered what else to take, I heard a whistle upstairs, signalling that the dinghy was waiting. As I rushed up on deck, I bumped into Petyo, who, like me, had been wondering which cameras to take and how many spare rolls of film. Henro had foresightedly told him to get ready at

MEETING *ARGO*

once and to accompany me aboard *Argo* to record our meeting with Tim Severin.

Argo's dinghy ferried us over in a matter of seconds. Peter, one of the British rowers, the one I'd spoken to the previous day, came over to help us climb aboard in the stern, since the swell tossed the rubber dinghy high up and away from *Argo* each time we tried to get a foothold on her.

From that moment on everything seemed like a film to me. My mind kept filling with images of the way I had envisaged things would be, what *Argo* would look like and my meeting with Tim Severin, and these mental pictures kept juxtaposing with reality. The result was something like a dramatised documentary, in which I was both an actor and at the same time a viewer watching the episode and wondering what would happen next. At first, my subconscious brought out pictures of Tim Severin's other boats as I had seen them on the covers of books: the *Brendan*, made of hide, with the huge figure of Trondur Patursson, a yachtsman and artist from the Faroe Islands standing in the bow taking a practice swing of his harpoon; then his picturesque medieval Arab dhow *Sohar* which Tim used for the Sindbad Voyage, its impressive sail billowing to the backdrop of an oil platform off Singapore; and now here I was, aboard his third ship *Argo*; I felt as if I was reading his as yet unwritten book, *The Jason Voyage*, and had somehow become one of its heroes.

Tim Severin still had his back to me, since he'd been manning the steering oars while we boarded *Argo* and was proceeding to change tack. A breeze had just sprung up again, and the galley was moving under both wind- and muscle-power. Some of the crew were still swinging the oars, with exclamations in Anglo-Georgian, and some of the enormous Georgians were obviously having trouble confining themselves to the cramped space of the rowing-benches, constantly banging

145

their backs against the oars of the men behind them. A few of the English and Irish crew were walking up and down between the bow and the stern and milling around the mast sorting out the innumerable sheets, barely able to pass one another on the narrow gangplank that led between the rowers' benches. After almost three months aboard, just one word from Tim Severin was enough for them to know which sheet to tauten among the apparent tangle of ropes on the deck.

As I watched all this, I exchanged a few words with Peter, who was in the stern. Had they had any problems so far? In the first stage of the voyage, going through the Bosphorus had been the most difficult bit, for which they had to tack from the European to the Asian side and back again, making use of the counter-currents that existed close to either shore. Then rough weather in the Black Sea had broken one of the steering-oars, and Peter only just managed to patch it up to get them into port. After Sinop they were caught in a storm which had swept them out to sea and broken the other steering-oar, and it was five days until they managed to dock at Samsun. The local papers had even had loud headlines proclaiming: 'British Sailors on *Argo* Lost in Black Sea!'

While chatting with Peter, I kept on watching Tim, who was giving the Argonauts instructions on how to position the sail in order to get the most out of the wind. Then a large man with a friendly smile on his face and a white peaked cap on his head turned towards me:

'Hello, Theodor!' boomed the basso of Yuri Senkevich. 'Well, how're the Bulgarian Argonauts?'

Yuri had heard about our expedition as a member of *Vokrug Sveta*'s editorial board. After Yuri, Tim Severin turned around, leaving someone else to take over, and offered me his hand.

'Welcome on board *Argo*!'

I thanked him, and presented him with the Orpheus carving.

Naturally he immediately looked at it with curiosity, and this allowed me to skip the opening formalities and to say:

'We heard that you were missing one of the ancient Argonauts in your crew, and since he was a Thracian musician we decided to bring him, at least in symbolic form, aboard *Argo*.'

'Orpheus!' Tim smiled. 'He played an important role on the Argonauts' voyage. And it wouldn't have been bad if we'd had someone aboard to soothe the storms and the waves with music.'

Tim took the figurine, and, as I explained to him the symbolism of its different elements, he started to stroke the lyre with his hand.

'What wood's it made of?'

'Lime.'

'It's got a very noble aura. Please thank the sculptor on my behalf! It's a pity that Trondur, our artist, isn't here; he'd have been glad to see this, but this week he had to go to the Faroe Islands for an exhibition he's holding there.'

While Tim spoke, I looked at him closely. A thin figure, not very tall, with a quiet, studious manner, not even the beard he now wore brought him close to the image of the famous mariner we obtain from books. But the moment he started talking about his expedition, his light-coloured, sharp eyes lit up brightly, and one could immediately sense the determination of a man who believes in his work and who is completely engrossed in the subject he has chosen to investigate. When I handed him the file of articles by Bulgarian archaeologists and historians, which I had put in waterproof sleeves, I was immediately aware of his approving smile. It was a real pleasure to observe his keen interest in everything: where exactly the ingot had been found, what the ancient name of Cape Kaliakra was, whether similar ingots had been found on the Bulgarian coast, what different kinds of stone anchors had been found off the Bulgarian coast and where the stone came from, who was responsible for submarine archaeology in Bulgaria, what the Bulgarian branch of the UNESCO Scientific Expeditions Club was engaged in . . .

'And who made *Argo*'s stone anchor?' I asked.

'We had consultations with a famous British archaeologist, Honor Frost, who pointed out to us a specimen that was commonly used in the Aegean during the Mycenaean age. I now remember that she said something about a particularly rich collection of stone anchors from one of your Black Sea ports – I can't remember its name, but she had been there.'

'That must be Sozopol, or Apollonia Pontica in ancient times,' I replied, showing him one of Misho Lazarov's articles. 'You'll find more details about stone anchors in here; it's a study by the scientific head of our expedition, who knows Honor Frost. She came to the international symposium on Thracia Pontica that was held in Sozopol.'

The sound of wood cracking and loud cheers interrupted our conversation. One of the Georgian rowers had taken to his role as a Greek hero so much that in his enthusiasm he had cracked the thick pin that held his oar in place.

'That hasn't happened until now,' said Tim, laughing, 'and, of the ancient Argonauts, only Hercules could have managed it.'

Someone elbowed me in the ribs mischievously. It was another one of the Georgian oarsmen whom they called Jackie. He winked at me:

'We trained for *Argo* with heavy oars, so now these ones seem as light as feathers to us!'

I looked at him in awe. Those 'feathers' were at least four metres long!

This interruption brought me back to earth again, and I looked around to see what Petyo was doing. He was in his element now – walking around the galley, jumping over the oarsmen, crouching down to photograph all kinds of details.

'When are we going back aboard *Aurora*?' he asked.

I shrugged my shoulders. Our yacht was sailing quite close to *Argo*. Henro was at the helm and had been watching us carefully, for he raised his hand in greeting the moment I looked over towards the yacht. Tim Severin, seeing that we were worried, made us an offer we couldn't refuse.

'I'll send some of the boys and the TV crew over to your yacht, and hope that you will stay here on *Argo* for the entry into Poti.'

Petyo and I looked at each other dumbstruck. We hadn't expected a gesture like this! The two expeditions entering Poti harbour together for the official welcoming ceremony – we hadn't even dreamed of it!

But Tim Severin himself could hardly have guessed what was in store for him in Poti. Far ahead of us, *Tovarishch* entered the harbour, showing us the way. A few of the Argonauts started tidying up the galley, as far as this was possible, by shoving their utensils and supplies under the benches, and coiling up the ropes in proper naval fashion. Then they all grabbed their oars. The Irish started singing a song which was designed for the rhythm of rowing, while the Georgians joined in the chorus. The sea for its part joined in with the noise of the seething, oar-struck water.

When we got into the waters of Poti, the Argonauts' song was drowned out by the cheers of the waiting crowd, and then by the sound of all the sirens of the ships, motorboats and hydrofoils moored up in the port. Everywhere was black with people, not only in front of the Sea Terminus, where *Argo* was supposed to moor up, but along the whole length of the harbour, in the boats all around and in the cabins of the harbour cranes. As we approached the Sea Terminus, we heard with growing clarity through the general noise the stirring harmonies of traditional Georgian folk choruses. The only bit of free space, evidently the spot where the modern Argonauts were expected to land, was cordoned off by a Georgian male-voice choir, all of them wearing the traditional costumes of long black coats, silver cartridge-cases on their chests and white headscarves which hung down to their shoulders. In front of them stood several voluptuous Georgian girls, wearing transparent gold-threaded veils held in place by exquisite diadems, mother-of-pearl necklaces and long golden dresses gathered together at the waist by small brown belts. The Argonauts, who were rowing with their backs towards this magical sight, started craning their necks around to have a look. But in doing so they lost the rhythm of the oars.

'Watch your timing! Keep your eyes in the boat!' shouted Tim, who had taken command again, but only the Georgian rowers obeyed his second command.

Petyo had remained beside me in the stern, and when *Argo* was a few yards from the quay he ran over to the bow to throw a line ashore, shouting at me to throw one over from the stern. They were caught on shore, and soon the galley was tied up to the quay, and the Argonauts stepped out on to the soil of ancient Colchis.

The Georgian fiesta ensued with such giddy rapidity that photographers and cameramen were at a loss as to where to aim their lenses. A crowd of children showered us with flowers, the Georgian girls brought us wine and fruit, the choir was singing at full blast, the mayor of Poti welcomed the Argonauts to the land of the Golden Fleece, and Tim Severin also made a speech, obviously moved by this hearty, colourful reception.

Among the smiling faces all around I also saw the members of our crew – *Aurora* had docked first so that Tim Severin's camera crew could film the landing. Nikola Gigov also appeared, content among the tumultuous festivity. The crowd surged forward to take a closer look at the galley and nobody wanted to go, although the Argonauts themselves had gone off for lunch. When they got back, Tim informed me that they were immediately setting off up the river Rhioni to try to get seven kilometres upstream by late afternoon. We also set sail aboard *Aurora*, along with a number of other yachts to see *Argo* off to the mouth of the Rhioni. The galley would be the only craft able to continue upstream, though, because it could sail in five times shallower water than our yachts, and it could also lower its mast to help it fit under the bridges that crossed the Rhioni.

The sea-water was a greyish-yellow colour at the mouth of the Rhioni. We followed *Argo* more closely than the remaining yachts, not noticing them when they retreated back out to sea.

'Come on, let's take her about!' Henro called. 'There are probably sandbanks around here.'

His words were confirmed as the yacht juddered to a halt. There *were* sandbanks.

For more than an hour we watched *Argo* labour upstream and gradually vanish among the reeds and bushes that had provided such good cover for the original ship, according to Apollonius. But at that moment the last thing Henro, and for that matter all the rest of us, wanted to hear about was Apollonius. *Aurora* simply refused to be separated from *Argo* and head back into the open sea, even though she couldn't proceed any further upstream because of the shallows. Henro had to send Stoyan and Petyo out with the anchor in the dinghy to try to free the yacht from its position in the shallows and get to deeper water.

After this unexpected exercise, the captain decided that we'd had enough 'experimental marine archaeology', that we'd seen enough of that 'low-lying barge' and that it was high time we set sail for home. I maintained a tactful silence until we arrived back in Poti harbour. I hoped to get a lift in one of the press cars to the spot upriver where *Argo* would land, so that I could finish my conversation with Tim Severin. Then we really would be able to head for home.

But we were too late. All the cars which had official permission to visit *Argo*'s camp had left. Alarmed by the huge crowds of curious visitors that had gathered in Poti harbour, the organisers had decided to limit access to the upstream camp lest the famous Georgian hospitality became too much for Tim Severin and his Argonauts. What could I do?

I decided that only a sailor would be able to help us in this situation, and so Sergei and I went straight to the harbourmaster; we needed a car with government registration plates. We didn't have to do much explaining. Ten minutes later, we were driving inland towards the seventh kilometre, wearing all the cameras we had, the flag of the UNESCO Scientific Expeditions Club with the Argonautica Expedition emblem flying on the bonnet for greater authority.

We got there barely in time. *Argo* had just thrown anchor, after making her way under the low bridge over the Rhioni with her mast lowered, continuing under oars. Small motorboats bustled around *Argo*, ferrying the Argonauts ashore.

Tim Severin was the last to come ashore, and was immediately besieged by journalists. It was clear that I wouldn't get the chance to speak to him here, but I had to try to make an appointment for the evening. As I approached, he noticed me and waved.

'I haven't forgotten! On the way up I only managed to glance at the titles of the articles. They look very interesting, and I've got the folder with me now,' he said, opening his travelling bag to reveal our file beside a soap-box and a towel. 'It's a good thing you put them in waterproof folders, because we're off to the baths now, and that looks like the only place where I'll be able to look at these things in peace. We must see each other again this evening.'

'Where?' I asked.

'I'm not too sure of the programme myself. I only know that there'll be an official dinner with the mayor of Poti. Where will you be?'

'At the Sea Terminus where *Argo* landed today.'

'Good. I'll find a way of dropping by your yacht before dinner. 'Bye for now.'

Sergei and I were just about to turn back, when a familiar voice called us. Valery Chaprava had also come to met Tim Severin and with an enigmatic smile told us that we were now honorary members of the Argonauts' Club. Sergei and I looked at each other.

'That's the first time we've heard about such a club!'

'The main thing is that they know about your Argonautica Expedition,' Valery went on, indicating a man of venerable age beside him. 'May I introduce to you the president of the Argonauts' Club, the historian Vianor Pachulia, candidate-member of the Academy of Sciences.'

The name rang a bell. Then I remembered that in the last weeks before setting off we had sent a letter to the magazine *Travel in the USSR*, which was the equivalent of our magazine *Discover Bulgaria*. The editors replied, saying that in Georgia we would probably meet up with Vianor Pachulia, one of their contributors.

We returned to Poti with Vianor and one of his colleagues, an archaeologist who was a personal acquaintance of Misho Lazarov's. Vianor was an interesting man to talk to. He had been on submarine archaeology trips in Suhumi Bay in search of the ancient city of Dioscuria. Classical authors claim that it

THE ARGONAUTICA EXPEDITION

was founded by the two Argonauts Castor and Pollux, also known as the brothers Dioscuri, after the Argonauts had found the Golden Fleece.

'And what is this Argonauts' Club?'

'It was set up at the beginning of this year in Suhumi, and its members are scholars, researchers and writers who are working on the Argonauts. We started collecting information on the subject from various Soviet and foreign museums and libraries, and also organised an exhibition entitled, 'On the Track of the Argonauts'. Georgi Zagrafopoulo, a Greek from Suhumi and an experienced shipwright, made a special model of *Argo* based on ancient Greek descriptions. We plan to build a research boat for expeditions around the shores of the Black Sea.'

In Poti we took Pachulia and the archaeologist to meet Misho Lazarov aboard the yacht. Vianor was greatly disappointed to hear that we would not have time to sail over to Suhumi, but that we would have to hurry along the Asia Minor coast to get back on schedule.

'Then we can arrange a special visit for you to our Argonauts' Club in the future. Where's your skipper, so we can make arrangements now for another voyage?'

Henro had vanished mysteriously together with Petyo and Stoyan, despite his previous impatience to get going 'as soon as possible'. I walked up and down the quay twice before I heard his hearty laughter. It was coming from the yacht *Ajaria*, which had also gone to greet *Argo*'s arrival. Looking into the cabin through the hatch, I realised that we wouldn't be setting sail so soon, after all. Our crew was captivated by the lads from the Batumi yacht, and at the moment they were exchanging elaborate toasts and gifts: 'To the crew of *Aurora* from the crew of *Ajaria*! Thanks to Tim Severin for our meeting! *Gaumarjos!*'

Henro seemed to have forgiven Tim Severin, experimental

MEETING ARGO

marine archaeology and all, and gave a generous wave of the hand when he finally noticed me standing by the hatch.

'The whole evening is yours! Give Tim my regards, and tell him I hope he finds his Golden Fleece, but not to forget Medea. He seemed to be a bit up in the clouds, like all you scientists – all those Georgian girls throwing themselves at his feet, and him rushing off up the Rhioni. You'd think the river was going to dry out by tomorrow . . .'

'It won't dry out!' concluded Stoyan, deep in thought.

'Well, he's not like old Stoyan here, is he?' Petyo said. 'That's all he ever thinks about, isn't it?'

'And so should he!' retorted Stoyan. 'Otherwise how's he going to get the Golden Fleece? We're not going to falsify history now, are we?'

I left them to develop their friendship with the Georgian yachtsmen, because Valery had come to call me, saying he knew where we'd be able to find Tim. In Valery's car, which seemed to be more or less of Argonautical vintage, we managed to get to the town park, where the Phasis National Academy was. There was going to be an improvised concert in honour of the new Argonauts. As we threaded our way among Potians in festive clothing, we stumbled across Nikola Gigov. He evidently hadn't been wasting his time either. He introduced me to his companions – I fell into the warm Georgian embraces of Akaky Tikharadze, chief editor of the newspaper *New Colchis*, and Georgii Gurjia, curator of the Poti Local History Museum.

'Any idea when the concert for the Argonauts begins?' I asked Nikola's new friends.

'But it's just finished!' they replied, looking at me in surprise and clapping their hands in disappointment. 'Tim Severin and his lads have gone off to the Sea Terminus, where there'll be an official dinner with the mayor.'

155

That was too much. While I'd been wandering around in the park, Tim had probably dropped by *Aurora*. I dragged Valery off with me and we got into his car, which strained with all its might to get us back to the harbour.

There was the sound of voices from both *Aurora* and *Colchis*, which were tied up together. Tim's Argonauts were sitting in the cockpit and chatting with the crews of both yachts. The centre of attention was, of course, the wife of *Colchis*'s skipper, a gorgeous and effusive Georgian woman, whose joy seemed to flow from her very being, and Yorrie, whom everyone called 'Medea' instead of 'Maria'. To my surprise, I heard her speaking English. To my even greater surprise, they seemed to understand what she was saying.

'What do you think!' she shouted at me, pleased. 'I even spoke to Tim. I managed to tell him that you'd be back soon.'

'And where is he?' I asked, looking around.

'He's down in the cabin,' Peter indicated. 'While we were all relaxing in the bath-house, he was so engrossed in some mysterious file that I was beginning to wonder if he'd found a Georgian edition of *Playboy*. But it was your articles. I never thought that Bulgarian historians wrote such interesting things! Tim's the only one who can read stuff like that in the bath without losing his concentration.'

I climbed down into the main cabin. Ilya Peradze had unfolded a detailed map of the river Rhioni, and was discussing with Tim what route *Argo* should follow. *Argo*'s final destination would be Vani, where archaeological excavations directed by Othar Lordkipanidze illustrated the entire course of Colchis's development. In the ruins of the ancient city, he had found a Greek shrine, or rather a shrine complex, which gave him reason to believe that this was the place meant by Strabo when he described the plundering of the wealthy shrine to the goddess Leucotea, or Hecate. And the high priestess of Hecate had been Medea. Some authors had suggested that Vani might be the legendary city of Aeae, Aeetes' capital.

But the symbolic finale for *Argo*'s voyage for Tim was the first town up the Rhioni where traces of the Late Bronze Age, i.e. the time of the Argonauts, could be found.

'You'll have to ask Othar Lordkipanidze himself about that,' said Ilya, shrugging.

'Well, we'll be together at the dinner anyway,' said Tim, looking at me. 'I managed to look through the articles by your historians, and I hope we'll have time to discuss them now.'

So we went out on deck for some fresh air. It was a fine, clear evening, the waves rocking *Aurora* gently, the breeze bringing cool, fresh sea air. I was on cloud nine – at last I had my chance to have a proper talk with Tim Severin.

I didn't suspect that there could also be a cloud ten.

Because just then two familiar figures approached the yacht in the darkness – Yuri Senkevich and Gerontii Kukhaleishvili, the mayor of Poti. They were coming to invite Tim and the Argonauts to their official dinner.

That was the last straw! Would we never get the chance to talk? After the dinner, which wouldn't be a hasty affair, Tim and his crew would be taken back up the Rhioni by bus so that they would be able to set off upstream early tomorrow. And that was when *Aurora* would be homeward bound for Bulgaria. What then?

Tim didn't leave me in limbo for a long time. He drew me in front of him and informed the mayor:

'This is a friend of mine who's the leader of the Bulgarian Argonautica Expedition, and I'd like to sit next to him this evening.'

Kukhaleishvili spread his arms out generously and gave a wide smile:

'Need you ask?'

And so I found myself on cloud ten. Which was actually a long festive table, with Tim Severin on one side, Yuri Senkevich on the other, and further down Professor Lordkipanidze, Gerontii Kuhkaleishvili, the crew of *Argo*... As we were taking our places, Tim reviewed his lads.

'Where did you get those T-shirts?'

They nodded in my direction. I realised that most of them were wearing white T-shirts with the Argonautica badge on them, the ones Petyo and I had given them when we had boarded *Argo* for the first time.

'They're just the job!' one of the Irish Argonauts laughed. 'All our clothes are dirty, and we were just wondering what to wear in Poti after our bath.'

'Why is there a lyre instead of a mast?' another asked me, looking at the emblem on his chest.

I explained to him the symbolism of Misho Peshev's design: Orpheus's lyre in place of a mast to catch the winds of inspiration.

'That's amazing!' exclaimed *Argo*'s photographer John Egan. 'I thought there'd be some interest in Jason and the Argonauts and in our voyage in Greece and here in Georgia, but I never thought that the Bulgarians would be interested.'

'Well, they're descendants of the Thracians,' Tim explained. 'And Orpheus is actually a Thracian musician, who later joined the Greek pantheon. That's why in *Argonautica* he appears mostly when the Argonauts are sailing past places inhabited by Thracians or tribes related to them. When I read the articles today,' he said, addressing me, 'I was interested to see that Orpheus might have been a real living figure in the thirteenth century BC, which was when Jason made his voyage to Colchis. I've always thought that there is some reality behind legendary figures, and that they are mythologised afterwards for religious and political ends.'

MEETING ARGO

Some of Tim's crew-members hadn't yet realised what we had given them on *Argo*, so I had to explain once more the symbolism of the 'strange wooden figure' we had presented to them.

'The moment at which you gave me the figure,' Tim said with a smile, 'was one of the best of the whole voyage, because it was so unexpected, and also because it came at a time when *Argo* was sailing along nicely, after all her adversities, towards her final goals, Colchis and Phasis.'

Of course, many more memorable moments awaited Tim and the Argonauts in Colchis – in Vani, Kutaisi and Svanetia, the main gold-mining region of Colchis, as well as in Tbilisi, the capital of Georgia. All this was hinted at by the mayor, who raised a toast, indeed a model Georgian toast, since at one point I was worried that the whole dinner would be over before the toast was. He spoke on in his sing-song tone, as if he had all the time in the world before him, and his classic finale showed that that was in fact the case:

'As you probably know, you are in the land of centenarians. Recently a Georgian at the peak of his strength – he was about a hundred years old – fell in love with a young girl. Only the mother's jealousy prevented the wedding from taking place, as she was only half the age of the groom. People live long here because their hearts are full of kindness. For this reason I would like to wish to Tim Severin that he lives long enough so that in thirty-three centuries' time, the same length of time that divides us now from the legendary voyage of the Argonauts, we will be able to gather again at the table. We for our part will guarantee our presence. To our future meeting. *Gaumarjos!*'

The mayor didn't forget to raise a toast to the health of our expedition too, mentioning that there had been rumours afoot in Poti that among us were direct descendants of some of the Argonauts, and that we had pictures of the Golden Fleece with us. There was nothing left for me to say in reply, except that our few days' sojourn in Georgia was sufficient to show us how legends were made – at our next meeting in thirty-three centuries' time, there would probably be a legend about how Orpheus brought the Golden Fleece back to Colchis.

That reminded Tim of our gold ingot from Kaliakra. He rummaged about in his pockets and got out the two colour slides of the ingot which I had included among the articles.

'I'd never heard of this ingot before. I've seen similar ones, except that they were made of bronze, like the famous ones found at Cape Gelidonya. But I haven't seen one like this, made of gold, silver, copper and other elements. If we assume that it originated in Colchis, would it have been possible for an alloy like this to have been produced here in the Bronze Age?' Tim turned to Othar Lordkipanidze for an answer.

'At that time,' the professor said, nodding, 'Colchian metallurgy was flourishing thanks to the introduction of a number of technical innovations. The main one was obtaining alloys of different properties. We have analysed metal items of the Late Bronze Age, and these analyses have shown that they have a varied chemical make-up.'

'And have ingots of the same period been found here?' Tim asked.

'Copper ingots,' the professor said, 'have quite often been found at great distances from their natural places of origin. That is why we assume that the original ingots were melted down again.'

'Were ingots used in Colchis as a means of exchange, that is in place of money, before the appearance of coins?' I ventured.

The professor looked at me:

'Yes, some scholars assume that as early as the Late Bronze Age massive copper rings, for example, as well as copper ingots, were used as a means of exchange. Others suppose that in Colchis before the era of Greek colonisation the means of exchange was gold in the form of standardised ingots. This claim is based on the gold and silver ingots found at Chuburiskhinji, which unfortunately haven't survived. But, for the time being, this is all in the realm of hypothesis...'

'Of course, just like our theory about the connection between the gold ingot and the Golden Fleece,' I said, shrugging.

Lordkipanidze smiled:

'I got the letter with your theory through Professor Velkov, and I agree with him about its legitimacy. Precious metals were obviously one of the things that attracted the ancient Greeks towards the eastern Black Sea. Later on the Greek towns in Colchis became trading colonies or emporia, based mainly on metal-mining in this ore-rich region.'

'And which of the different theories about the Golden Fleece do you accept?' I asked Tim.

'I think that the most logical one is the one Strabo gives when he describes the mountain regions of Colchis and Svanetia: "... the mountain streams carry gold, and the barbarians gather it using sieves and fleeces ... That is how they say the legend of the Golden Fleece arose." In my view it's difficult to give one single reason for the Greek drive towards Colchis. For instance, your theory about gold ingots cast in the shape of "golden" fleeces also has some grounds. It could be a consequence of what Strabo describes.'

'Apart from that, in Strabo's case,' Lordkipanidze went on, 'there is no doubt about the authenticity of his description. This ancient method of panning for gold was used until quite recently in Svanetia. Bochorishvili, one of our ethnographers, describes how the Svans, the inhabitants of the mountainous regions of what used to be Colchis, use sheepskins to extract gold from the river. They stretch them over wooden boards or something similar, and then submerge them in the river with the wool on the outside, fastening them so that they don't get taken away by the current. The wool traps the particles of gold. After a certain time, the fleece is removed from the water, spread out on the ground to dry, and then the gold-dust is beaten out of the wool. It's difficult to find a greater confirmation of the descriptions of ancient authors. In a couple of days you'll see it for yourselves,' the professor went on, turning to Tim, 'when we visit the river Inguri in Svanetia, which also carried gold, like the Rhioni. There are some old Svanetians there who will specially demonstrate the gold-gathering method using sheepskins. If you've come all this way on *Argo*, you must come and see the Golden Fleece.' Lordkipanidze narrowed his eyes, as if on an examining commission. 'Did you know that there are legends in Svanetia about the existence of a stone shrine with underground vaults in the Leshkhvara mountains? The vaults are said to contain gold treasures and a ram tied to a gold chain.'

Tim looked at him, intrigued.

'All I know is that, as far as I'm concerned, I've discovered the Golden Fleece I want,' he said laughing. 'And that is the information that I'm going to get in Colchis from you and the other Georgian archaeologists. I'd be very grateful if in the next few days, while we're together, you'd put me in the picture about the Late Bronze Age in Colchis from the excavations you've made and the studies of your Georgian colleagues. Our Jason Voyage has almost completed its purpose, which is to prove that it was physically possible for Greek ships of the Late Bronze Age to cover the route taken by Jason. Now, for the symbolic completion of the actual voyage, I'd like you to show us the first town upstream along the Rhioni where there are Late Bronze Age remains, so that *Argo* can anchor there.'

'That'll be Chaladidi,' the professor promptly replied.

'How far is it from the place we moored *Argo* this evening?' Tim enquired.

'About ten kilometres.'

'Fine. That means tomorrow we can row up to Chaladidi, moor up and use our remaining days to visit Vani and other archaeological sites that you will show us together. Anyway, I don't think that a stranger like Jason would have dared to venture very far upstream in an unknown land. Chaladidi then . . .' said Tim thoughtfully. 'That's an interesting coincidence, because I asked the Georgian rowers, who are familiar with the river, where they thought the best place to stop was without risking the galley too much, and they said that they wouldn't go any further upstream than the Chaladidi region. And they weren't thinking of Bronze Age sites, either . . .'

'Too much talk,' Yuri Senkevich's deep voice intervened. 'And we're falling behind with the toasts. *Gaumarjos!*'

Again the toasts got going. I soon noticed Tim furtively trying to dilute his wine with a soft drink of the same colour so as not to offend his toasting hosts. He was saved by photographer John Egan, evidently one of the jokers of the voyage, who started getting to his feet at every toast, to enthusiastically yell, '*Gaumar* . . .', and then signalling to the other Argonauts to complete the toast, also on their feet, in chorus, '. . . *jos!*' This, of course, made the hosts feel obliged to get to their feet too, and in about quarter of an hour the physical effort started to dampen their desire for new toasts, and a relative calm ensued at the table. Tim and I were again able to speak.

'When I was looking through the articles by your researchers,' he began, 'I was specially intrigued by an article by Professor Velkov, who's the scientific director of your expedition. He's the only one of the authors whose name I knew from publications abroad. In the article, along with the development of underwater archaeology in Bulgaria, he mentioned mutual influence among the cultures of the Black Sea during the Bronze Age. Would you ask Professor Velkov to send me some more Bulgarian studies on migration in the Balkans at that time? Classical authors, for example, mention that some tribes from northern Anatolia migrated to the Balkans. Is there any evidence of such migration from the region of ancient Colchis and northern Anatolia towards the Balkan Peninsula?'

'I think that the president of our UNESCO Scientific Expeditions Club, Vladimir Popov, will be able to help you there. He's head of Sofia University's Centre for Ancient Languages and Cultures, and that's right in his line.'

'What interests me is the possibility that the Aeolids, Jason's family, had connections with the people of Colchis. That's the only explanation I can find for the fact that the people of northern Greece once knew about the ram cult in Colchis during the Late Bronze Age, which is what archaeologists are beginning to reveal now. It's interesting that the same thing must have occurred to Apollonius, because he hints at it in Jason's words to Medea when he tells her that the people of Iolcos don't know about the "Isle of Aeae", even though the Aeolids were supposed to have moved to Greece from Colchis. And this again would indicate the possibility of some tribes from the eastern Black Sea migrating to the Balkans, bringing with them the myths and traditions of their region.'

I tried to think back through what I had read in preparation for the Argonautica Expedition without getting bogged down in too much detail – this wasn't the right place for it. So I told Tim that Bulgarian scholars had rejected the previous hypotheses of an Indo-European invasion from the north assimilating the non-Indo-European population of the Balkans. The latest hypothesis was of a general process of Indo-Europeanisation in the Caucasian region of the Black Sea, Anatolia, the eastern Mediterranean and the Balkans all at the

MEETING ARGO

same time – without, of course, excluding the possibility of migrations. In fact, it was considered that the process of Indo-Europeanisation in the Balkans was hastened by the coming of other Indo-European tribes from the Black Sea area. And the people whom Homer called Achaeans, who included the Argonauts and all of the tribal groups that spoke early Greek, which has been provisionally designated as Mycenaean, were assumed to have come from Asia Minor in the east. I also told Tim about some of the more interesting Late Bronze Age finds in the Balkans – briefly, because on the other side I could see Professor Lordkipanidze looking on with a smile as I enthusiastically went about publicising the achievements of Bulgarian archaeology.

'I think,' said Tim, turning to the professor, 'that in the coming decade Balkan archaeology will be the most productive field for explaining the history of the second millennium BC. That's where the major answers lie!'

I only regretted that Misho Lazarov wasn't with us. Lordkipanidze, who knew him well, asked me about him, but he had gone off somewhere with his Georgian counterpart Vianor Pachulia just at the time when Tim and the mayor had invited me to dinner.

And dinner appeared to be coming to an end, as could be seen by the dishes arranged on top of one another, nobody having any strength left to reach out for the food. 'That's what I imagine medieval feasts must have been like!' groaned Peter Moran, *Argo*'s Irish cook, depressed at the sight of so much food that could have kept the crew of the galley going for several days more.

'When are you sailing home?' Tim asked me as we were getting up from the table.

'Tomorrow morning, when you start taking *Argo* further up the Rhioni.'

'What will your course be?'

'We're more or less taking the same route as the Argonauts did according to Apollonius. But we'll be continuing to the western Black Sea of course, without entering the Danube.'

'When you get back to Bulgaria, could you send me something about the greatest difficulties that face a boat going upstream along the Danube?' Tim asked. 'Are the Iron Gates a big obstacle? That is, would they have been in ancient times? For instance, many scholars claimed that a galley from the time of the Argonauts couldn't have sailed up the Bosphorus, but *Argo* has proved them wrong. Would the same thing go for sailing up the Danube? And, more important, is there any practical possibility of a ship such as *Argo* getting to the Adriatic Sea following one of the tributaries of the Danube, as Apollonius says? Along the Sava, or some other river, for example? What do you think?'

'I very much doubt it. A friend of mine from Plovdiv, Hristo Bliznakov, has sailed a lot on the Danube and in other rivers in the Balkans and Europe. I mentioned the return route described by Apollonius to him when we were preparing our expedition. I was thinking of it as a further stage of the expedition, but Dr Bliznakov was highly sceptical. He said that it would definitely mean hauling the boat overland at one point, somewhere in the mountains of Yugoslavia, between a tributary of the Danube and a river that flows into the Adriatic. It might be possible with a rubber dinghy, but one couldn't possibly drag a galley like *Argo* across.'

'Yes, it's practically impossible, isn't it?' Tim agreed. 'I've read descriptions of boats being carried overland in some parts of the region between the Baltic and the Black Sea, and came to the conclusion that such operations were exceptionally difficult. Travellers preferred to carry their baggage in the usual

MEETING ARGO

way, and then build small boats when they reached a convenient river. Originally I had the intention of coming to the Balkans and looking for possible sites where the Argonauts might have transferred from the Danube to get to the Adriatic, but I'm becoming increasingly convinced that there simply isn't a route, and that Apollonius must have got his geographical facts wrong.'
'What do you intend to do, then?' I said, asking the question which interested me most of all.
'As far as I'm concerned, the end of the Jason Voyage is here in Georgia, and the Argonauts' return route could be the subject of a separate expedition. It's a difficult question, which includes additions from Ulysses' voyage made by various authors. It's difficult to see what has been taken from Ulysses and ascribed to the Argonauts and vice versa. Actually, next year I intend to follow Ulysses' route from Troy to Ithaca. I think that there'll be room among the crew of the new expedition for a descendant of the Thracians...' Tim said, looking at me enquiringly, with a faint smile appearing at the corners of his mouth as he noticed the mixture of surprise, delight and disbelief on my face at this totally unexpected proposition. After all, no Bulgarian had ever taken part in such an international expedition before, and I thought that I'd be the last person in the world who would have the honour.

I glanced at Yuri Senkevich. I wondered how he had felt years back, when he had first learned that he had been chosen for Thor Heyerdahl's crew.

But it was time for us to part. Before getting on the bus that was to take them to their camp on the Rhioni, the Argonauts dropped by *Aurora* to say goodbye to our crew.

We gave the photographer John Egan a photograph of the gold ingot and he, in his characteristic manner, started shouting emotionally, waving the photograph about:

'The Golden Fleece! The Golden Fleece! Come on, let's thank Medea!'

And they all lined up to give Yorrie a kiss.

Then Henro opened *Aurora*'s log, and Tim Severin wrote in it, 'I wish the Argonautica Expedition success – it was wonderful meeting in Poti!'

9

HOMEWARD BOUND

The next morning *Argo* continued up the river Rhioni towards Chaladidi.

Aurora weighed anchor to sail from Poti back towards the coast of Asia Minor. Our new-found friends from Poti came to see us off, some of them accompanying us to the harbour bar in small boats. Zaza was among them, and he waved after us for a long time, sorry to see us going so soon.

Tim Severin had been right: the return journey could be the subject of a separate expedition, or even several.

If Jason's voyage in search of the Golden Fleece reflected some real event, regardless of whether it had been a one-off expedition or the opening of a new sea-route to Colchis, we can consider that the original version of the myth ended in Colchis. About the return journey there are as many different stories as there are authors, who let their imaginations run riot on the subject. So it seems likely that the different stories of the heroes' adventures on their way back originate from a later date and reflect the geographical knowledge of different periods.

Some of this knowledge was probably related to the assimilation of new trade routes in the Black Sea. That was why we wanted to use *Aurora*'s return journey to follow part of the Argonauts' return journey as Apollonius Rhodius described it.

In his account, they left Colchis on a fair wind, which could have been the strong *Abaza* which blows off the Caucasus to the shores of Paphlagonia, in present-day Anatolia. Then they stopped by the river Halys, which is designated on modern maps as Kizilirmak, at which point they parted with the coast of Asia Minor, leaving Cape Carambis (today Kerempe) to the south, and cutting straight across the Black Sea to the Istros, or Danube.

'Neither the heavens nor the winds abandoned the mariners until they reached the Istros,' Apollonius tells us. This strengthened Misho Lazarov's belief that the ancients did not limit themselves to coastal sailing, but were able in fine conditions – with a clear, starry sky and a fair wind – to take short cuts across the Black Sea.

We, too, intended to effect such a crossing with *Aurora*, except that we would call in at Trabzon, Samsun and Sinop before heading into the open sea. They were the ancient seaports that Misho was interested in seeing. The local inhabitants say that there are only four safe harbours on this coast of Asia Minor: Samsun, Trabzon, July and August. As it was late July, we would have the chance to try out all four 'harbours'.

The first of them, July, did not seem very reliable. We didn't enjoy the same fair wind as the Argonauts had. As soon as we got on course for Trabzon we encountered a head wind, and were kept busy tacking all day. It got stronger towards evening, and succeeded in snapping the Genoa jib-sheet. It looked as if we were in for stormy weather. The yacht was heeling badly, with the waves breaking over her gunwale. Every time we went about, the danger of ripping a sail or a foresheet increased, so Henro lengthened the tacks even if it meant going slightly off course and heading out into the open sea for a while. He ordered shorter night-watches so that those on watch wouldn't doze off. We hadn't slept properly the last couple of nights because of all the excitement of meeting *Argo* and Tim Severin.

We got into bad, frequent waves which buffeted the yacht side on, making her heel badly and hitting her again and again before she could right herself. Our stomachs were turned inside out after the Georgian feasts. Sergei and Misho rushed to their bunks as soon as their watches were over, in such a hurry to lie down that they hardly had the patience to take their waterproofs off in the swaying cabins. Yorrie didn't sleep in her bunk in the forepeak, where the waves hit hardest. She slept the whole night out in the cockpit in the ceaseless spray. Henro and Stoyan regularly checked the lines, as far as this was possible, to make sure we'd have no broken sheets or halyards, which in our circumstances would have unforeseeable results. Petyo tried to establish our position – not by the stars, but using the radio direction finder set, so that we could head for Trabzon again once the wind died down.

And it did die down in the morning, but the sea itself took longer to become calm. It continued to rock us all day long, to the accompaniment of the unpleasant shivering of the limp sails on the spreaders and masts.

Only on the second night did we see the shore lights and the intermittent flashes of Trabzon lighthouse. Henro was apprehensive of entering a strange Turkish port in darkness, and so we decided to stay adrift until daylight. We even managed to get a bit of sleep, leaving only one man on watch for eventual changes in the current, another ship or an approaching patrolboat. Tim had mentioned a slight counter-current when he had sailed *Argo* along this section of the coastline, but it would be in our direction, and, if we got into it, it would only take us to Trabzon. There were few ships in this region. We didn't even see a patrol-boat until daybreak, when we entered Trabzon's Fakliman Harbour. Henro was offended by this indifference towards our yacht, and started calling the border control over the radio. Nobody answered, and so finally we set off to find the harbour police office ourselves and have our papers checked. In the office they looked at us in a daze as we explained who we were and where we had come from. Later, we found out that *Aurora* was the first foreign yacht to call there that year. In the end they got themselves together, and the whole lot of us drove in cars down to the yacht, picking up the port doctor on the way, who also wanted to witness this rare event. Now Henro could no longer complain about being ignored. We were given the complete treatment, with all the pomp and frills, and we were even issued with a Shore Pass – a document which is usually issued to big ships. It allowed us to go ashore within the town limits, provided we were back on board by nightfall.

But there wasn't really anywhere to go late at night in Trabzon, which is not a tourist town. Picturesquely situated on a number of hills, it does offer something for those interested in antiquities; it is advisable to visit them by day, though, because a careless step on the unlit ruins of the city walls or the once magnificent palace of the medieval Comnenus dynasty could easily result in a sprained or broken limb. Hovels made of the same stone now huddle around the erstwhile palace. The story goes that once a local governor asked who this Comnenus was, and saw no reason for maintaining his huge residence if he didn't pay any dues or taxes. And since then the once magnificent building has served as building material for the houses around.

As we wandered about the ruins, Misho Lazarov gave us a brief outline of the history of Trabzon. The first settlement on this spot is believed to have appeared in around 2000 BC, and in the eighth century BC the Greek colony of Trapezos was founded there. Its name came from the trapezium-shaped plateau on which the citadel stood, cut away by the river gorge. The Greek historian Xenophon tells us that the city had been subordinate to Sinope.

'Do you remember me telling you about the emperor Hadrian in the museum at Kutaisi?' Misho went on. 'Hadrian doubled the size of Trapezos by building walls in the lower part of the city which reached from the castle to the sea, and also built an artificial harbour. The stone blocks of the harbour wall were set in a curve, and they can still be seen today from the site of the citadel.'

'Yes,' I said, 'when I told Tim that we were going to go back via Trabzon, Professor Lordkipanidze said that Trapesund, as it was also called, had some connection with Colchis. What was the connection?'

'Trapesund came within the borders of historical Colchis. In the Kutaisi Museum, I also told you about the geographer Arianus, who was sent on a trip around the Black Sea coast by Hadrian. Both he and Xenophon before him described the tribes living in the Trapesund region as *Colchi*. One of the Colchian tribes, for example, was known as the Macronae. Anyway, let's go and take a look at the museum.'

Somebody had told Misho that there was a museum in Trabzon with pottery fragments from the Bronze and Stone Ages which strongly resembled similar pieces of the same period found off the Bulgarian coast. So we tried to find the whereabouts of the museum, stopping people in the street and asking: 'Museum? Musée? Muzeisi? . . .' But all we got in reply were confused shrugs and answers of '*Yok!*' Misho started losing patience. 'What do you mean, *yok, arkadas*? There's got to be a museum here! Moo-ze-um. Ce-ra-mic . . . Ke-ra-mik . . . An-tik . . .' At which the people looked at him in even greater confusion. At long last, someone's face lit up:

'Aya Sofia!' he replied.

'We're not from Sofia!' Henro retorted. 'Varna, Varna! Only woman from Sofia,' he said, pointing to Yorrie, and then, pointing to me, said: 'And he's from Filibe! I won't tell them about Sergei, because it'll get too complicated . . .'

The man looked fearfully at Henro, towering over him with his bearded face and giving him a lesson in Bulgarian geography in his booming voice, repeated 'Aya Sofia!', pointing to the west, and hurried on his way.

'Only heard about Sofia,' Henro muttered. 'At least he knows which direction Bulgaria is.'

'It seems to me that he's referring to a church of St Sophia,' Petyo intervened hesitantly, and decided to put his knowledge of Turkish to use after our futile attempts in English, French and German.

He seemed to have quite a decent vocabulary, because the next passer-by we stopped immediately confirmed his words:

'Aya Sofia *Muzeisi*!' And added: 'Hagia Sofia Museum', again pointing westwards, in the direction of the seafront.

'Of course, he means the Church of St Sophia!' said Misho, slapping his forehead with his hand. 'I've heard that it's the best-preserved Byzantine church in Trabzon. The museum is probably next door to it.'

We had to walk practically the whole length of the town in order to reach Aya Sofia. The museum turned out to be the church itself, which contained some magnificent frescoes. It had been built in the thirteenth century by Manuel I, who was head of the Trapezund Empire which was founded after Byzantium had split into several parts. Manuel I was a pretender to the throne in Constantinople, and had evidently decided to build a church to rival the splendour of St Sophia's in that city.

On the outside parts of the apses, we noticed paintings of sailing-ships. We found out that these represented the large two-masters of the Trapezus fleet, as well as smaller Venetian traders. The vessels were probably painted when the ships were launched or before long voyages by sailors or shipowners to bring them good luck. But there was no pottery of the kind we were looking for in the museum. Misho leafed through various reference books and brochures at the small gift-stall in the churchyard, but there was no mention of 'old crocks', as Henro called them.

'I must have been misinformed,' shrugged Misho. 'Perhaps they meant Samsun.'

'Or Sinop,' Henro said. 'We can look for museums up to there, but if they meant Istanbul, you can forget it.'

In the evening, exhausted by our day's traipsing around, we returned our passes to the harbour police and returned to our yacht, which was in Fakliman harbour. Several fishing-smacks and tugs had tied up beside *Aurora*, and their crews were all squatting around her mahogany hull. She was evidently an unusual sight in this harbour.

'How's it going, friends? Make a big catch?' Petyo asked them in Turkish. That was enough to win their sympathy and for them to invite us to an improvised supper of fresh fish on the quay beside the next fishing-smack.

We produced some rakia from our diminished supplies, and the conversation flowed smoothly. It was conducted partly with Petyo's help, partly in Anglo-Bulgarian, and in 'nautical language', which consists of hand-gestures and common words which have remained the same among all who sail the Black Sea. We realised that the crew of the smack next to ours had just called in at Trabzon after Samsun, and were here temporarily. At one stage Henro scrutinised their rocking vessel:

'Hey, Petyo, I can't see an aerial anywhere. Ask them if they have any kind of radio transmitter.'

Their captain, a wiry but broad-set man, with a short black moustache and deep furrows on his face, nodded in negation: '*Yok!*'

'And do they use an RDF set?'

Another nod of the head.

'So how do they find their bearings?'

'Simple!' said the mustachioed man with a sweep of his hand. 'We sail out into the *acik*, the open sea, far from shore, then we turn west and then we get to Samsum.'

'Yes, but how do you know where you are?' Henro persisted. 'Do you use a compass, or log?'

'*Kafa*, captain, *kafa*,' the man laughed, tapping his head with his hand. Then he attempted to explain to us how, for instance, by the small clouds that appear in the east over that hill there, by the colour of the sunset and by other signs of that kind, tomorrow we would have a relatively light breeze, which would continue all night and only strengthen tomorrow afternoon. If we set sail tomorrow at noon, we'd have calm sailing until the evening of the following day. But after that, the wind would blow up strongly.

'He must have been born at sea!' Misho exclaimed, slapping his knee in enjoyment. 'There you have centuries of seafaring knowledge handed down the generations.'

Our conversation went on till late at night. Misho was tired of gesticulating, but managed to ask the experienced captain about the local currents in this part of the sea, the prevailing winds in each season, and other ways of forecasting the weather. He was most interested to hear that in the old days sailing-boats crossed the narrowest part of the Black Sea, from the region around Cape Bafra, Inceburun and Cape Kerempe, over to the Crimea.

The following day we decided to take the advice of the fishing-boat captain and set sail at noon. There really was a light breeze behind us. Stoyan was itching to raise the spinnaker, something he hadn't had the chance to do for a long time. During the first night, the sailing was easy. The hilly Turkish coast proceeded slowly to port, with the lights of villages showing here and there: Besikduzu, Gorele, Tirebolu. We approached the place which Tim Severin had identified as the isle of Ares described in *Argonautica* by Apollonius. It is today the uninhabited island of Giresun, situated near the town of the same name, known as Cerasuntus in ancient times.

On Ares, the island belonging to the god of the same name, Jason met four young men who turned out to be his relatives. They were the sons of Phrixus, whose father Athamantus had been the brother of Creteus, who was Jason's grandfather. These four sons were the result of Phrixus's marriage to Chalciope, King Aeetes' daughter. On his death Phrixus's last wish was that they sail to Orchomen in Greece, his birthplace, to seek their inheritance. So the young men had set off on a Colchian ship, but had been washed ashore by a storm at Ares.

An interesting point about this significant encounter is that it suggests that ships sailed along a fixed route between Colchis and Greece before *Argo*'s voyage. Apart from that, there is the fact that on one shore of the Bosphorus the Argonauts had met the Thracian king and soothsayer Phineas, who had given them precise information on how to proceed along the southern coast of the Black Sea to get to Colchis, mentioning also the island of Ares.

But, before meeting Phrixus's sons, a further trial awaited the Argonauts on the island. It was inhabited by the stymphalydes, copper-winged birds which fired their feathers like arrows at people. The Argonauts had to don their helmets and hold their shields over their heads, and in the end frightened the birds away by shouting and banging their weapons on their shields before landing.

Tim Severin believes that this episode might be a reference to the vast flocks of birds that inhabited the island, just like the island of Giresun. When Tim and his Argonauts anchored on Giresun in the modern *Argo*, whole flights of seagulls and cormorants had flown up into the air and circled for a long time over these intruders to their kingdom. In this connection, Tim had told me: 'I always prefer the simple answer, if there is one.'

But now that answer seemed too simple for Misho, who told me about his friend Alexander Snisarenko and his interpretation of the Argonauts myth. Snisarenko had said that the episode with the stymphalydes had been an ornamented description of the Argonauts' encounters with the Colchians, the most powerful and warlike tribe on the whole coast from Trabzon to Poti. Using as his basis the island's name of Ares, the historian from Leningrad turned his attention to the different meanings of the Greek word *arete*, the meanings of which range from 'skill' and 'ability' to 'bravery', 'strength' and 'might', all of which applied to the Colchians, who were known not just for their military prowess but also for their metal-working skills, in particular gold-working. Hence, Snisarenko concluded, there must have been metal deposits on or near Ares, and therefore the mysterious island's location should be sought somewhere off the coast between Hopa in Turkey and Batumi in Georgia.

Apollonius described several tribes with unusual customs inhabiting the part of the coast we were sailing past. Among the Tibareni, for example, it was customary during childbirth for the men to lie down on their beds and groan instead of the women, while the women fed them and cared for them as if they were the new-born children. The Mosynches were named after the huts they lived in, and they did in public what others did in private, including love-making.

Herodotus also mentions that tribe. But most numerous

references among Greek authors are made to the Chalybes, a tribe who mined metal. Apollonius locates their territory as being near the territory of the Tibareni, who lived to the east. They made their living not by farming or herding, but by extracting ore from the 'bowels of their iron-yielding earth'. Their flotational method of extracting iron has been revealed by archaeologists as being common in the south-western regions of Colchis.

When *Aurora* was off Yasunburun, Misho Lazarov told me that the name of the cape probably commemorated the Argonauts' visit to the Chalybes, and meant 'Jason's Cape'. The wind was still with us, but a strong swell had risen against us which lifted the ship's rudder out of the water and forced it around, making steering increasingly difficult. To Stoyan's chagrin, we were forced to lower the spinnaker, as the wind was gradually getting stronger. The skipper of the Trabzon fishing-boat had been right, then. In the evening an even stronger wind blew up, and Henro ordered us to raise the storm-sails, just in case. We flew past the low shore at the estuary of the river Yesilirmak, mentioned by Apollonius as the Iris, and as we rounded Cape Civa, we saw with relief the lights of a big town – Samsun!

It was after midnight when we sailed past the green blinking light into the big harbour. We sailed around the harbour once to find a suitable mooring-place, but finally tied up to another vessel for the night. The wind whistled through the rigging, the halyards slapped against the masts like overtightened guitar-strings. We were just dropping off to sleep when a strong squall hit the yacht and the fenders creaked ominously against the side of the neighbouring ship. This happened a few more times during the night, and in the morning we found the whole deck of the ship covered in dust. If the gale had been so strong in this protected harbour, what would it have been like in the open sea. The men on the next boat told us that at midnight they had heard gale warnings over their radio, and that later in the night the winds had reached force 8 on the Beaufort scale.

In Samsun port formalities were over quickly, possibly because this was a yachting harbour. We were told that there was a yachting marina there, and so we promptly moved *Aurora* to it. We were warmly received, were helped in replenishing our water-supplies, and were able to have a bath – our last bath had been a week earlier in Poti. Sergei was just wondering what to offer us in the way of meals other than the monotonous tinned food, mainly peas and beans, when we were invited to dinner at the yacht club. We found the table laden with steaming plates of . . . beans. But they had been cooked with all necessary condiments, and were accompanied with side-dishes of cucumbers, tomatoes, lettuce and a huge juicy water-melon for afters.

We emerged from our bath wearing clean T-shirts with the Argonautica emblem on them. When he saw us and heard that we had met Tim Severin in Georgia, Osman Silahcioglu, one of the committee of the yacht club, showed us into the guest-room, where there was a photo of *Argo*, with Tim's familiar signature beneath and the date, July the seventh, written below it. Osman was an energetic young man and himself the skipper of a wooden yacht which he proudly showed us. His friend Hilmi Gurlar was no less enthusiastic on the subject of sailing. He was retired, and was now dedicating all his time to building a new small wooden yacht. In the club workshop, Hilmi showed us the unfinished hull of his yacht, as well as his models of old boats, smacks and fishing-boats which were arranged on the shelves around.

'That's an *alamana* over there,' said Hilmi, showing us one of the models, 'which is typical of part of our Black Sea coast. I think it's the one that's most like the hull of *Argo*. I've asked

HOMEWARD BOUND

Severin to send me a copy of the plans of the galley so that I can make a model of it to put beside the *alamana*, just for comparison.'

Misho Lazarov was pleased. Here was further confirmation of what he had been looking for, of seafaring skills being handed down from generation to generation. If we traced their development back in time, we would reach the era of the Argonauts and find that the resemblance between *Argo* and the *alamanas* and *maunas* that had existed until the recent past was not accidental. Vasilis Delimitros, who had built the modern *Argo* on the island of Spetses, had evidently retained the traditions of the Greek shipwrights. Hilmi also stated that he knew old people who could build *alamanas* using the traditional methods. In fact, he himself had repaired *Argo*'s steering oar without using nails, the same way Vasilis Delimitros had done, after it had snapped during a storm between Sinop and Samsun.

'There must be old shipwrights living in Bulgaria who can build ships like that,' Misho said with determination. 'And sailors to sail them!'

'It's possible,' Henro agreed. 'But it was only when Tim came to the Black Sea all the way from Ireland for his experiments that we realised that we've got shipwrights and sailors, too. It's always like that. While we sit around twiddling our thumbs, someone else overtakes us. Because if someone'd had the idea of building a galley in Bulgaria, a dozen institutes and scholars would probably have spent years wondering whose design to build it after, who should head the scientific team, who would oversee it, who would finance it, what the result of the whole project would be and, finally, whether to build the thing in the first place.'

As I studied the model *alamana* in Hilmi's workshop, I wondered why *Argo* bore the most resemblance to this kind of traditional craft. Tim Severin and Vasilis Delimitros had built this galley using as their basis ancient Greek pictures of ships from the Late Bronze Age. But why had tradition preserved the hull dimensions of this particular type of boat? What were they used for? It occurred to me to ask Hilmi if he had any idea where *alamanas* had been most commonly used at the time when they were powered by sails and oars and not by engines.

'Mainly the Sea of Marmara and the Bosphorus,' he replied. 'Because of the strong currents there, they made their hulls long and narrow.'

That explained things to a large extent. The seafaring tradition which Misho had talked about had probably retained certain kinds of hull as most suitable for dealing with the strong currents in regions like the Dardanelles, the Sea of Marmara and the Bosphorus – all of them important obstacles to be overcome in the voyage of the *Argo*.

We didn't have to look long to find a museum in Samsun. Near the marina a fair was being held at the moment, and we went to it, attracted by its oriental bustle and colour. We grabbed our cameras and, while we gazed at the stalls which offered practically everything, we found ourselves in front of a small building with a sign saying 'Archaeological Museum'.

There was pottery in this one, but not of the kind that Misho was after. It consisted mainly of amphorae from ancient Paphlagonia, west of Samsun. At the time of the Argonauts, the Paphlagonians were already inhabiting the Black Sea's Asia Minor coast, as they had done for more than five hundred years. There were also settlements in the Samsun region, at Tekekoi, for instance, where archaeologists have unearthed tombs from the Late Bronze Age. Their finds included bronze spear-heads, knives and earrings. The fact that Tekekoi had been a major settlement might have meant that in this area was the ancient trade route connecting the Black Sea coast with the

Hittite cities deep in Anatolia. On the way, as we were passing this section of the coast, Misho had mentioned that contacts between the Hittites and the Black Sea deserved deeper study. And the finds from Tekekoi confirmed this.

Samsun also stood on the site of an ancient city, Amysos, which had emerged after the sixth century BC when the Miletans captured it from the Phocaeans and founded a colony there. The city traded with Colchis, as we can see from Amycan coins discovered in Kobuleti on the Georgian coast, where we had met up with *Argo*. Strabo, who ought to have been familiar with the place where he was born, mentioned that the journey by sea from Phasis to Amysos and Sinope took two or three days. It had taken us that long to get from Poti to Samsun aboard *Aurora*, but an ancient ship would only have succeeded with the wind behind it. Some scholars have considered Strabo's figures to have been miscopied, with 2 and 3 written instead of 8 and 9.

As well as real ancient civilisations that existed in the regions around Samsun, classical authors also cited the region as the territory of the mythical women-warriors, the Amazons. As Apollonius says, after passing the river Iris, today's river Yesilirmak, and rounding Cape Themiscyra, today Cape Civa, the Argonauts anchored at the mouth of the river Thermodon in Amazon territory. If they had lingered there, they would probably have had to face the Amazons in battle, but a good wind blew up and they set sail from the shore where 'the Amazons of Themiscyra were preparing for battle'.

Both Herodotus and Aeschylus knew the region of Themiscyra. The river Thermodon was probably today's river Terme near the town of the same name, east of Samsun. Could the ancient name Amysos or Amasia, as the modern Turkish *vilayet* is called, be an echo of the word 'Amazon'? However, this was not the only place where the ancient Greeks located the beautiful but warlike Amazons. The regions where the Amazons were supposed to have lived cover a wide geographical range: the shores of Meothides, today's Sea of Azov, Scythia, Lesbos, Samothrace, Phrygia, Caria, Illyria . . . As the Greeks' geographical knowledge broadened, so the homeland of the Amazons was pushed further and further away, to places like Libya and Ethiopia, for example. In this way they always existed on the edge of the then-known world. I remembered my talks with the scholar Ivan Marazov before our expedition. He said that we could accept this constant distancing of the Amazons' homeland as indirect evidence of the fact that their original homeland had been Thrace. In other words, they had been Thracians in the earliest mythological stratum. 'The mythological existence of the Amazons is often associated with ancient Thrace,' Marazov had claimed. 'Sometimes the Thracians encounter Amazons while travelling and have to fight them, or they are allies in war, or some Amazons are Thracian by origin, and sometimes even the whole tribe of the Amazons lives in south-west Thrace.' Marzov considered these references sufficient grounds for focusing his research on the links of the Amazons with Thrace.

The next leg of *Aurora*'s trip home, from Samsun to Sinop, was a lesson in ancient geography. It seemed that Apollonius, in order to make his account as true to life as possible, had given a detailed description of the southern coast of the Pontus according to the geographical knowledge of his time. He usually stuck to Herodotus's descriptions, even though Herodotus had lived only two centuries earlier, and the Argonauts eight centuries before Herodotus.

We left Samsun at noon, seen off to the harbour limits by Osman's yacht. We had been in Samsun for only thirty-six hours, and the weather had not yet settled after the storm warnings of the night of our arrival, but Osman had given us a detailed weather forecast and we hoped to effect our rather delayed crossing to Sinop without much incident.

In the evening we were off Cape Bafra, which is the mouth of the river Kizilirmak. Apollonius Rhodius called it the river Halys. It was there, 'on Paphlagonian shores, at the very mouth of the Halys', that the Argonauts stopped on their way back from Colchis. Medea made them make a sacrifice to the goddess Hecate. They left Dascylus here so that he could return to his homeland. He was son of Lycus, king of the Maryandines who lived in the regions around Heraclea Pontica, the place where we had first reached the shore of Asia Minor aboard *Aurora*. On their way to Colchis the Argonauts had been well received by the Maryandines, and King Lycus had sent his son to act as their guide and to mediate on their behalf when they encountered other tribes friendly to the Maryandines. On the way back from Colchis, Dascylus had to disembark at the mouth of the Halys, even though his country was much farther west, because this was the spot where the Argonauts had decided to leave the coast of Asia Minor and cross the Pontus direct for the Istros, or Danube.

As we sailed past the Kizilirmak delta I looked at the chart and wondered why Apollonius had chosen precisely this spot for *Argo* to head out into the open sea and towards the Danube. I again remembered Misho Lazarov's belief that the ancient navigators knew certain direct routes across the Black Sea. If this was one of those routes, and Apollonius had known about it, why, I wondered, did it start at the river Halys, and not some other place, such as Inceburun, which is the northernmost cape on the coast of Asia Minor?

I got out my copy of *Argonautica* and re-read the section dealing with Jason's voyage along these shores, both on the way to Colchis and on the way home. It was interesting that in neither instance Apollonius mentions Inceburun under any of its names, although he always mentions the Halys. It was obviously a more common departure-point for the ancients. And they would probably not have been aware that Inceburun is the northernmost part of the coast. Even as late as the first century BC, Strabo speaks of the established view that a ship could cross the Pontus without losing sight of land if it sailed from Cape Carambis on the coast of Asia Minor to Criu Metopon on the Taurician Peninsula, today the Crimea. Carambis, or Kerempe, and not Inceburun! A look at these two north-facing capes on the map was enough to reassure me that the difference in latitude between them was negligible, and would hardly have been noticed by ancient navigators without exact data and charts.

But what about the river Halys? One look at the chart was enough to show that it was the biggest river on this coast. But what did the ancients think? I looked through the geographical notes I had previously taken in preparation for the expedition. Herodotus described it as a river famous since ancient times. 'The border between the Midean and Lydian kingdoms was the river Halys... It flows upwards in the direction of the North Wind, and divides the Syrian Cappadocians on the one side from the Paphlagonians on the other. Thus the river Halys cuts off almost all the lands of Lower Asia from the sea which is found opposite Cyprus, up to the Pontus Euxinus.' Thus the estuary of such a well-known river could very probably have been the starting-point for ships bound for the open sea.

But Cape Carambis was just as well known in those times. Why had it not served as a starting-point for the Argonauts? I again looked at my coastal charts. One possible answer was that for an ancient galley the mouth of the Halys and the bay right next to Sinop would have been a more convenient place to prepare for a lengthy crossing in open seas than the bleak exposure of Cape Carambis. From the river, the sailors would be able to take on supplies of fresh water, as well as provisions. Still, was that the only explanation? I tried to picture myself in the place of a seafarer of ancient times who had to choose between Halys and Carambis as a starting-point for a voyage across the open sea towards the Danube. Which place would give him more reliable bearings for the direction in which he should head?

So I looked at my general map of the whole Black Sea. I remembered Tim Severin's words about always preferring the simple solution. So, if I had to sail across to the Crimea without a compass, I would probably have chosen Cape Carambis to start off from. From there, all I would have had to do would be to sail away with the shore directly behind me, and keep on going in the same direction, something which presented no difficulty to sailors in ancient times. But as a point from which to head for the Danube I would probably have preferred some place around Halys, where the natural curve of the coastline in a north-westerly direction would be a guide as to which direction to head in. Keeping in this direction would take me across the Pontus to its north-western coast, and thus I would reach the estuary of the river Istros.

All my conjectures were, however, grist to Misho Lazarov's mill. He was more convinced than ever that a single voyage was not nearly enough to research the ancients' navigational abilities, and what was needed was a series of experimental voyages to study coastal landmarks, currents, winds and anything else a sailor might have used to navigate in that period.

For the time being, however, we decided to leave crossing the Black Sea without a compass to some future expedition, and jumped out on deck to give the watches their oilskins, since it was beginning to rain. Dark clouds rolled over the sky from the Anatolian coast and covered the stars. This was hardly the sort of weather in which an ancient vessel would have put to sea...

All night it continued to rain, and after my watch I wriggled into my sleeping-bag in the forepeak and immediately dropped off. Two or three times I was startled by the crash of waves breaking over the gunwale – my head was no more than a foot from the outside of the hull upon which the waves were venting their fury. In my half-dreamy state I imagined for an instant that I was in an open galley without a deck into which the waves could break unhindered, but immediately banished the image, endlessly thankful to be under *Aurora*'s secure deck.

When I woke up in the morning for my next watch and looked out through the hatch, I saw that we were entering a picturesque harbour with scores of fishing-boats of all sizes tied up to the quay, ruins of city walls along the coast and the variegated roof-tops of houses covering the hills beyond. We were in Sinop.

The rain had eased off temporarily, but it soon started drizzling again. The gusts of wind, which were growing stronger each time, and the rising swell, could worryingly be felt in the harbour, which was situated on the southern edge of an isthmus jutting out eastwards, on whose rocky back the town was situated.

We didn't feel like going out anywhere so early on this rainy morning. It was obvious that in such weather we would be stuck in Sinop for at least two days, so that there was no need to hurry. We boiled up some tea and took stock of our provisions, since from here we would head out into the open sea for the crossing to Varna.

A few hours later, when the rain eased off again, a crowd of curious bystanders appeared by *Aurora*. Here, too, a yacht flying a foreign flag was a rarity. Henro remembered being given a message from the Samsun yacht club for a friend of theirs here, who went by the nickname of Habesh. As soon as we mentioned the name there was a buzz among the onlookers on the quayside, who started nodding their heads affirmatively and pointing to a fishing-boat on the opposite side of the harbour. But there was no need for us to go looking for him. Quite soon a fit-looking man, well into his fifties, wearing a sailor's shirt beneath his yellow waterproof anorak and a sporting yachtsman's čap with a huge peak, appeared next to *Aurora*. His English was quite good, not in a grammatical sense so much as in the wealth of words and phrases which life itself had evidently taught him. He told us his real name, which none of us remembered, because we insisted on calling him Habesh, as everyone else did. Habesh means something like 'Blackie', a name which had been given him ever since he was a child because of the dark colour his skin had become through his spending so much time out in the sun. He was a fisherman and skin-diver and now had that fishing-boat in the harbour, which he had also christened *Habesh*, and he often helped yachtsmen like ourselves who happened to put into Sinop.

Henro handed him the note from the Samsun yacht club and invited him aboard.

'Just a minute, let the harbour police come first,' he said, nodding to a shed at the far end of the quay, at the same time smiling at us and shrugging as if to say that formalities were formalities.

The harbour police were already emerging from the shed, together with customs officers and the harbour-master. The usual procedures followed: passports, stamps, signatures . . . Where were we coming from, where were we going, why had we stopped in Sinop, what were our professions? They were impressed by Misho Lazarov's profession, 'archaeologist', and started guessing exactly what he did as an archaeologist until he told them that he was also a lecturer in history. They called him 'the Professor', and looked at him with particular curiosity – what was he doing here messing around in boats with these lads? He must be a wealthy man to be able to afford cruises like this. So he wished to see the museum, did he?

Habesh did his job as translator successfully. He had difficulty only in explaining to us that for the time being just two of us could go ashore – for bread, water and provisions, while the others would have to remain aboard; there were further formalities for which the policemen's boss would have to come.

So Misho and I set off with Habesh, who showed us to the shops on the waterfront. We asked him if we would only be able to go ashore in twos like this.

'When the big boss comes he'll probably sort things out,' said Habesh, looking almost apologetic. 'It's because of the Americans,' he went on, looking up at the hill.

On the hill sparkled two large white spheres, probably some kind of radar equipment. We should have remembered! Captain Dremdjiev, who had entered the same harbour aboard the yacht *Vega* ten years earlier, had told us that we could expect more than the usual formalities in Sinop because of the American military base there. And *Aurora* was probably the first ship flying the Bulgarian flag to put in here after *Vega*.

We came back with bread and vegetables, and let the next pair go off to the main street, to replenish the water supplies. Half a day passed in 'walks' like this, until finally the 'big boss' himself appeared in a car. He was told who we were and why we were there, and we were informed that we could go sightseeing in the town as long as we didn't go to 'that hill'.

'What do we want that hill for anyway, to pick grapes?'[1] Henro retorted, which gave us a problem as to what to translate, until finally Habesh said something to the effect that we

---

1 This is a reference to the Bulgarian idiom 'I don't need a vineyard on the hill', meaning 'I'd better steer clear of this.'

didn't need a hill, but some of the good local wine, which resulted in a smile from the 'big boss' and the good disposition of his subordinates.

'And the museum?' Misho asked impatiently. The museum was shut today. But it seemed that we would still be there tomorrow, judging by the weather, which showed no signs of improving. The wind was still whistling in the mainstays and blowing grey clumps of cloud across the grim sky.

In the evening Habesh really did bring home-made wine along, with fried grey mullet. We got talking and found out that he had lavished the same hospitality on the crew of *Argo* about a month before. That was probably why, when I had asked Tim Severin's Argonauts which Black Sea town they had liked most, they had all replied 'Sinop!' Habesh laughed in satisfaction when he heard this, his eyes sparkling in his suntanned, weather-beaten face. 'That is what I like doing now – helping seafarers like you and Tim Severin whenever I can. I've raised my children, I've got grandchildren now, so what do I need to save up money for? I'm a millionaire anyway, I have a million friends!'

The next morning Habesh again came with his hands full – this time he brought us half a tray of sweet, juicy baklava. After breakfast he accompanied us to the museum to show the amphorae he himself had brought up from the bottom of the sea, sometimes diving to a depth of 60 metres to get them. Some of them were displayed in the fine park in which the museum building stood. We were really pleasantly surprised: both the park and the museum were spick and span and everything had been professionally arranged. Now Misho couldn't complain of not having any ceramics to look at. The pottery covered a broad span of time during which life had continued uninterrupted in Sinop; in fact, the region was one of the first inhabited regions of Anatolia. In the nearby village of Demirci finds from the Early Bronze Age, around 3000 BC, had been unearthed.

Before our visit to the museum, I took another look at the second song of *Argonautica* to see how Apollonius Rhodius had described this region. He wrote that the Argonauts stopped on 'Assyrian shores', a name which authors in ancient times used to describe the areas around Sinop. These areas had been inhabited by Leucosyrians, and so the whole region was known as Leucosyria. The original name of Sinova, which later changed to Sinope, is believed to have been given to the settlement by the Assyrians, whose documents contain the earliest records of the Colchian tribes of Georgia and their land by the Great Sea, as the Assyrian conqueror Tiglatpalasar I called the Black Sea. Apollonius also mentions the name Sinopa. Sinopa was a girl who came to live in these lands at the will of Zeus. Zeus had wanted to 'commune with her in love', promising first to give her what her heart desired most. The crafty girl replied that what she desired most was her virginity, and thus she put an end to the advances, not just of Zeus, but also of Apollo and the river-god Chalys. This is probably the legend of the foundation of one of the earliest Greek colonies in the Black Sea, although Apollonius does not mention the city itself. This, according to the traditional chronology, emerged only after the voyage of the Argonauts. Modern historians date its original foundation to the eighth century BC, although soon afterwards it was destroyed by the warlike tribes of the Cimherii, who destroyed the first Greek settlements in the southeastern part of the Black Sea as they migrated to the northern coast of Asia Minor around Sinope. About a century later, Greek settlers from Miletus resettled in Sinope, and, while during its first period of existence it had functioned mainly as a base for coastal navigation, this time it became one of the main colonies of Miletus in the Black Sea, gradually subjugating

Trapezus and Kerasunt. Some scholars even believe that it played a role in the colonisation of Colchis in order to have some influence in this ore-rich region. Amphorae from Sinope have been found in various parts of Colchis, including some which Othar Lordkipanidze unearthed in the tomb of a famous warrior in Vani. He has found two further locally made amphorae there, and the fact that their design is based on those originating in Sinope shows how pottery from Sinope influenced Colchian pottery.

Another interesting fact was that in the episode where Jason stopped in Assyrian lands *en route* for Colchis he came across Greeks who had arrived there before the Argonauts. They were the sons of a certain Deimachus from the city of Trici in Thessaly, the same region which *Argo* set sail from. They had dropped out of Hercules' campaign against the Amazons, and now were glad to rejoin their countrymen. This encounter strengthens the impression that, even before the Argonauts, there existed established overland and sea routes which enabled the Greeks to get to the Asia Minor coast of the Black Sea.

I was now interested in seeing in the Sinop museum what kind of tribes had inhabited these shores in the Late Bronze Age and may have been met by the Argonauts. I was helped by the museum's curator. On learning that we had met Tim Severin, he told me that during *Argo*'s stay in Sinop he had taken Tim to see the remains of a settlement from that period. It was situated on a hill several kilometres from Sinop, and its inhabitants had been the mysterious Kaskas tribe, which appeared around 1800 BC according to Hittite records. Presumably a trade route had linked the Hittite capital Khatusa in the northern part of central Anatolia with the coastal regions of Anatolia by the Black Sea, where the Kaskas lived, as this was the shortest outlet to the sea from the Hittite capital. And, indeed, only recently Mycenaean pottery had been found in the remains of a palace at Khatusa. Greek jars from the time of the Argonauts in the Hittite capital! Could they be evidence of maritime links between the Mycenaean Greeks and the Hittites, a route passing through the Bosphorus and along the southern coast of the Pontus to the Kaska lands around Sinop?

Misho Lazarov got Petyo to take photographs of the pottery vessels in the museum so that he could compare them with those found in Bulgaria. He looked in every nook and cranny of the museum for a stone anchor or at least a shaft, but in vain. Evidently the amphorae were the only direct evidence of ancient maritime traffic here. Then Habesh took us to the northern part of the isthmus so that we could see the remains of Kumkapi Kalezi, the main gate of Sinop's waterfront walls. The original walls are believed to have been built by the Kaskas. They were afterwards repeatedly destroyed and rebuilt by Greeks, Romans, Byzantines and Seljuk Turks. A plaque placed here by the archaeological trust told us that the walls were mentioned in Hittite records. Even today the half-ruined walls, collapsing into the sea, still retain some of their original grandeur. About 30 metres high, they girded ancient Sinope for some two kilometres, with mighty watchtowers at regular intervals, the remnants of which are also to be seen today.

The northern shore of the town provided the best view of the sea, although at the moment it wasn't a pretty sight. Foaming crests could be seen as far as the horizon, and when they reached the shore they hurled themselves furiously at the base of the ancient walls, their spray sometimes shooting all the way to the crenels at the top. The wind came in gusts from the west, bringing with it salty spray which it carried all the way to us on shore. Habesh wrapped his waterproof more tightly around him and shook his head:

'The way he's rebelling now, Karadeniz won't let you go for another day at least.'

And he was right. The next day Henro, Habesh and I took several walks along the waterfront to see what Karadeniz, or the Black Sea, was doing – and it was certainly living up to its name.

I remembered what Strabo had written about the Pontus in Homer's time: 'At that time the sea was unnavigable and known as "the inhospitable" (Axinos Pontus) because of its storms and the savage tribes inhabiting its shores . . .' If in his *Odyssey* Homer spoke of *Argo* as a famous ship ('everyone knows it'), then Strabo's words about the Axinius Pontus would apply equally strongly to the time of the Argonauts. Some scholars believe that the Greeks may originally have associated the name Axenos with the toponym Axshaena, an old Iranian word denoting the dark colour of the sea. That was what the Scythians, who inhabited its northern shores, called it. The Phoenicians subsequently altered the name to Ashkenas, which they later used to denote the Scythians and possibly all peoples living to the north. In this sense, Ashkenas probably also meant 'Northern Sea'. But the Greeks then could have interpreted this name in their own way, using the Greek word *axenos*, 'inhospitable', to replace Axshaena and Ashkenas.

Only on the third evening did the wind abate, the clouds disperse and the swell calm down. We started preparing the sails. Habesh came to say goodbye, and asked Henro when we intended to set sail.

'Perhaps at daybreak, perhaps earlier,' said Henro uncertainly.

'You're the captain, so you decide,' Habesh responded. 'But let me give you a piece of friendly advice. Rest for a while now, and raise the sails at midnight, when the offshore breeze starts blowing. You can't be sure of a favourable wind after that.'

Henro took his advice and at around midnight we left Sinop,

carefully rounding the peninsula and passing Inceburun, after which we pointed the yacht towards Cape Kerempe. The breeze really did help us, as Habesh had predicted, but at about four in the morning the wind changed direction and started blowing against us.

We spent all day tacking along the hilly coastline, heading out to sea in a north-westerly direction on one tack, and then shorewards again towards the whitewashed houses of places like Aiancik, Catalzeitin and Abana on the other. Towards evening we saw the lighthouse of Inebolu, after which the wind died down, until at two in the morning we were just off Cape Kerempe, almost totally becalmed.

Apollonius had described Carambis as a cape situated opposite the Great Bear, indicating that in ancient times the cape really did serve as a coastal bearing for true north. Apollonius also described another one of its features: the 'whirlwinds of Boreas', i.e. the north wind, were said to circle above it before going off in different directions. Watching the high coastline on either side of Kerempe as we inched past it, I began to see the logic of this. The north winds which blow at the cape probably turn into whirlwinds on hitting the mountain massifs, with some of them blowing eastwards towards Inceburun and Sinop, and others blowing westwards and south-westwards along the coast towards Eregli. So the head wind we had been encountering all day fitted in with Apollonius's description of this section of the coast. We could therefore count on the wind being behind us after Kerempe, at least initially.

And that is what happened. At daybreak there was an easterly breeze which gained in strength at about noon, gradually changing direction to south-east, which meant it was exactly behind us as we were now in the open sea, parting with the coast of Asia Minor for our last leg across to the Bulgarian coast. After Cape Kerempe the next cape we would see would be one of the Bulgarian capes Emine, Galata or Kaliakra, depending on which winds picked us up in the sea.

The fair wind continued all day long, and even into the night. There was almost no swell, and we couldn't dream of better sailing weather. Stoyan spent all his time around the spinnaker braces, as if performing a sacred rite over them, pulling the barely noticeable ballooning spinnaker to one or the other side at the slightest hint of change in the wind direction. We were all in the highest of spirits, especially on the next day when the sun wasn't covered once by cloud. After our rainy days in Sinop and the overcast sky that accompanied us towards Cape Kerempe, the sun started to shine through the clouds, and now we were really sailing not in the Pontus Axinos but in the Pontus Euxinos, the hospitable sea. It was high time for what the Turkish sailors had said about the 'four safe harbours' to come true, at least for August, since July hadn't acquitted itself very well in its role as such a harbour.

Sunshine, a fair wind, the sea ruffled lightly by waves – everything was so pleasant on the last day of our expedition that I suddenly felt a pang of regret as I watched the happy faces of the crew members and thought that from tomorrow onwards we would no longer be Argonauts. It would be back to the daily grind, with the expedition to Colchis gradually fading away into a distant memory of something which might not have happened at all – like the myth of Jason and the Golden Fleece.

What had we been looking for on the voyage? What had the Golden Fleece been for each one of us? Between the last watches, I managed to find time to speak with everyone separately.

Henro was pleased above all at having got to know the yacht in different situations – it had been her longest voyage yet – and at sailing the coast of Asia Minor, which few Bulgarian

THE ARGONAUTICA EXPEDITION

yachtsmen knew about. Successful, too, had been the experiment of a mixed crew consisting of yachtsmen from Varna and members of the UNESCO Scientific Expeditions Club from Sofia, as well as an archaeologist who was everyone's senior and had never sailed in a yacht before, but who had stood up to the adversities along with the rest of us. 'My greatest reservations about the whole expedition concerned taking aboard people who didn't know each other and might not get on, but they proved to be unfounded. I think that we could undertake even longer expeditions with a crew like this,' Henro said. 'And the most exciting moment of the whole trip for me was when you and Petyo climbed aboard *Argo*; it showed how important our expedition was and how important it was to Tim Severin, too.'

That was undoubtedly also Petyo's greatest moment; he had never expected to step aboard *Argo* at such a key moment, just as she was about to arrive at Colchis. 'It was a great chance for me to sail in this part of the Black Sea and to take photographs, which not every photographer and yachtsman is able to do. Oh, there were the occasional moments when I worried, of course,' he said with a smile. 'Things like whether Sergei would add bay-leaves or peas to our meal, or whether Stoyan would do his spinnaker trick again, but those were enjoyable moments.'

Stoyan was quite laconic: 'I enjoy sailing, and that's been my best experience so far.'

Yorrie, who had been through all the doubts and hopes of preparing the expedition with me, was now unstinting in her praise for the whole trip: 'I'd sail to the end of the world with a crew like this! I've never had a better time in my life, but to be honest I don't believe that a trip like this one can be repeated. As for Tim Severin, I never thought he would pay so much attention to us.'

To Misho Lazarov the whole journey was still a bundle of

theories that had to be sifted through, sorted and tied in with other evidence. 'I already consider myself ready to draw up a more concrete programme for studying ancient navigation, because now I'm more convinced than ever that a single voyage would not be sufficient,' he said. 'What it would require is a number of experimental voyages along hypothetical navigation-routes in conditions as close as possible to those of sailors in ancient times. Now, for instance, we're crossing the Black Sea again directly to Varna, the way sailors have been doing ever since ancient times – I am convinced of that now. Of course, we're helped by the compass and the radio. But what did the ancients use? Which stars are the safest guides? How did they follow them? That is a question which can be put to the test. Otherwise I'm very pleased by this voyage because it's the first time I have felt the atmosphere of the open sea, so far from land. Personally, it was a test for me, both physical and mental. I hope that I passed it and didn't cause the others too many headaches!' Misho smiled, nodding in Stoyan's direction: 'He'll be able to tell you best, because we were on watch together. As for our meeting with *Argo*, what was most interesting for me was to see how they worked the rectangular sail, how they used the winds, to what extent they could sail with a lee wind, and not only downwind, because ancient records of this are too general; they merely say that they sailed with the wind. And what pleases me most in our programme is that we got to see the Turkish coast. I think I'm the first Bulgarian or Soviet archaeologist to visit this coast. My overall impression is that, regardless of the specific development of the different nationalities around the Black Sea, you can see unity in the identical amphorae and pottery vessels in the museums, the similar construction of city walls, the similar forms of the ships, the names used for the winds, and the navigation systems. All this enables us to conclude that the

Black Sea has enabled the people inhabiting its shores to communicate through the ages. It seems that it's time for me to start writing a new book about the history of the Black Sea and ancient navigation.'

I managed to talk to Sergei only on our last night watch, because in the evening the wind had started to strengthen and change direction. We exchanged the spinnaker for the Genoa jib, which in turn had to be lowered, after which we were forced to lower the mainsail and continue on the smallest jib. There was a strong offshore swell which, together with the wind, made the yacht heel sharply leeward, with the waves breaking over her and pouring in streams off the Genoa jib, which had been lashed to the railings. Henro ordered all hands on deck, leaving Yorrie at the helm, while the rest of us rushed over to sort out the Genoa jib and one of the other jibs that had got tangled up in the railing on the other side. Then we fastened the mainsail to the boom even more securely, and looked around to see if there was anything loose or untidy left on deck. At that moment Petyo called out:

'Lighthouse ahead!'

We all looked in the direction he was pointing. Sure enough, straight ahead of us was the periodic flash of the lighthouse. Henro studied it for a while, and then recognised it:

'Kaliakra!'

Sergei jumped up and rushed to the bow of the yacht, repeating: 'Kaliakra, Kaliakra . . . that's where we are!'

The wind that had picked us up after Cape Kerempe had brought us across the western part of the Black Sea exactly opposite Cape Kaliakra, known to the ancients as Tyrisis.

Sergei couldn't keep still in his excitement.

'I had a feeling that we'd end up at Kaliakra. The Argonauts, too, must have sailed past Kaliakra as they sailed north towards the Danube.'

We joined him in the cockpit. The sea was still raging, but it slowly began to calm down as we changed course and aimed for Varna. Sergei was silent, staring, as if in a trance, at the flashing light of the lighthouse as it gradually fell behind us to starboard. Then he turned to me:

'Remember what I said to you last year when we were returning from Malta? It was a night watch again. About the ancient ship that was homeward bound with its cargo of gold ingots along one of the Black Sea shipping lanes, past Kaliakra. Now that I've seen *Argo* in Colchis, it all seems even more likely to me. Imagine a galley like *Argo* which, like us, is coming downwind from the coast of Asia Minor, and using Cape Tyrisis in daylight to keep its bearings. But as it approaches, it runs into bad weather. And so our ingot sinks to the bottom of the sea. It needn't even have been a shipwreck. If the galley was heavily loaded, with its gunwale low and near the sea with the waves swamping it, they may have had to jettison some of the cargo to make it lighter.'

'When I spoke with Tim Severin and Professor Lordkipanidze in Poti, they agreed that there could be some connection between our gold ingot and the Golden Fleece – on a purely hypothetical plane, of course.'

'I'm pleased that it will also arouse interest in other places. For example, they're going to put a photo of the ingot in the museum at Poti and in the Argonauts' Club in Sukhumi. I intend to do analyses in parallel with Georgian scientists of the ingot and of gold found in Colchis. We'll have to look out for similar finds, whether in Georgia or elsewhere. Perhaps that's one of the points we could bear in mind on our future expeditions, and study hide-shaped ingots from the Aegean, the Adriatic, Egypt . . .'

Future expeditions?

Day was breaking, and we could already see Varna's Cape

Galata in the distance. The Argonautica Expedition was coming to an end, and the memories of it were now bringing forth dreams of future expeditions. Where or when, we didn't know and didn't dare to predict. Nor did we dare to imagine the shape of the next Golden Fleece, the next great adventure that would fire our imaginations and not leave us in peace until we were finally underway. We only believed that the time would definitely come because whoever has been an Argonaut once is doomed to an endless quest for his Colchis.

In the morning we moored at the Varna seaport, tying up *Aurora* in the marina. People in holiday clothes crowded around us on the quay, the yachts around were crowded with people, and the training-ship *Kaliakra* was adorned with pennants as if for a parade. It was the first Sunday in August and the Week of the Sea would be officially opened. Pleased that we should return on this very day, many yachtsmen and friends of ours came to congratulate us on our successful voyage.

'Welcome home! How was it? Did you meet up with *Argo*?'

We were besieged by smiling faces, questions, cameramen and journalists.

Suddenly a friend whom I hadn't seen for a long time came running up. He was a sailor who was away on long cruises for months at a time. He smiled, waved and called:

'Good luck!'

The people on the quay started laughing, and he was told that we had just got back, and weren't setting sail like the other yachts, which were participating in a regatta for the Week of the Sea. He looked embarrassed for an instant, but quickly recovered and grinned:

'Well, good luck for next time then, because I might be away again the next time you set off.'

Of course, at that moment I didn't suspect that not a year would pass before I would set sail from the same harbour with another expedition, this time to the Aegean, from where I would continue on Tim Severin's galley for his Ulysses Voyage to Ithaca. But that's another Odyssey . . .